Praise for
The TEA SHOP

"Karl Forehand is a storyteller and theologian. In this remarkable book, he weaves together theological insights, personal experiences, and great wisdom for living life well. *The Tea Shop* takes readers on a journey of discovery that makes a difference!"

THOMAS JAY OORD, AUTHOR OF *GOD CAN'T* AND *THE UNCONTROLLING LOVE OF GOD*

"Karl Forehand has done it again! This time by sharing an intimate portrait of what he learned about the power of listening to wisdom from unexpected sources. Take some time to visit the Tea Shop with Karl and you'll be surprised at just how much you can learn from his mistakes and how much genuine wisdom can be acquired by admitting we don't know everything."

KEITH GILES, AUTHOR OF *JESUS UNDEFEATED*

"Karl's story is an insightful travelog of his soul's adventure as much as his Tea Shop experience in Taiwan. We think we would like to have an adventure, but then carefully plan it to maintain control. Real adventures only begin when the unexpected happens—whether that is a crash on a scooter, a last minute question about buying a tea pot, or a shaman-like owner of a Tea Shop where Karl discovered that 'love looked like a man with no name sharing his tofu with me.'

His spiritual adventure began much earlier with the crashing of the logical assumptions about where and how and through whom God would show up. Fortunately, he had eyes to see what Paula D'Arcy says so well: 'God comes to you disguised as your life.' May we all welcome the awareness of the unexpected presence of God in our everyday adventure."

DR. PAUL FITZGERALD, SPIRITUAL DIRECTOR AND
FOUNDER OF HEART CONNEXION MINISTRIES

"In this beautiful book, Karl helps us come into the now, the present moment—to slow down, to experience the experience we find ourselves in, and to somehow connect with the Divine in the midst of it all. We live in a fast-paced world where our desire to be in and out and on to the next thing can cause us to miss out on the beauty of the present moment; and in his book, Karl presents example after example of how to tap into the power of the mystics and just … be."

DR. GLENN SIEPERT, HOST OF THE
"WHAT IF PROJECT" PODCAST

"With the heart of a father, the mind of a mystic, and the soul of a pastor, Karl Forehand takes us on an extraordinary trip to Taiwan and to a Tea Shop with no name to remind and encourage us to be present in every moment of our lives. I loved every page of this book!"

"The wondering and wandering of Karl's journey is delightful. He takes a beginner's mind and shares how he sees the world. The questions and wisdom that follow are wonderful places to jump off into your own adventure. Thanks for sharing your story, Karl."

"As a Spiritual Director and fellow Souljourner with Karl, I deeply resonate with his honest, tender, and self-reflective story. Could real wisdom be the humility to always wonder if you're right? If so, Karl Forehand is a wise guide inviting us, through this book, to grow by allowing 'real intimacy and true healing' while humbly embracing mystery. These and more lessons from *The Tea Shop* are beautiful and timely for us all."

"Karl Forehand is one of my favorite humans. His authenticity and transparency immediately welcomed me into his 'inner circle' of friends at a time when I needed community most. The grace that marks Karl's life is deeply rooted in a mystical encounter with the radical hospitality and wholehearted acceptance of God that Karl experienced in a Tea Shop on the other side of the world. This book tells the fascinating story of what happened that day and how the ripples of that encounter have affected every day of Karl's life ever since. If you're longing to encounter that kind of divine embrace for yourself, set aside your preconceived notions of God and follow Karl into *The Tea Shop*. There is hope for every single one of us in these pages."

JASON ELAM, AUTHOR AND HOST OF THE
"MESSY SPIRITUALITY" PODCAST

"One thing about an adventure is that you can plan out ahead of time what you want to experience, but sometimes adventure has its own plans for you. An adventure can be life transforming whether it's two months or two weeks, or even two hours as it was with Karl. Join Karl on his epic journey in this engaging account of unexpectedly coming face-to-face with God in a most unlikely place and in a very surprising way."

JULIE MCVEY, M.S. FAMILY & CONSUMER
SCIENCES, AUTHOR OF *WHY I LEFT CHURCH
TO FIND JESUS: A PERSONAL ODYSSEY*

"When Dr. Seuss wrote, 'Oh, the places you will go...', he wasn't kidding! I have read many spiritual/theological books that reward me intellectually but this is a book that took me somewhere emotionally and spiritually.

In *The Tea Shop*, Karl Forehand takes us into one of the forgotten and oft-maligned aspects of Christianity: The Mystic. Mystical Christianity moves us from a mere religious experience to actually experiencing God. Karl also gives us some amazing insights based on his own spiritual journey and all he has gleaned from the spiritual journeys of others. Your cup of tea has been lovingly and patiently prepared and is eagerly awaiting you. Drink up!"

DERRICK DAY, SPEAKER AND AUTHOR
OF *DECONSTRUCTING RELIGION*

"Ever since I read the Tea Shop chapter in *Apparent Faith*, I've longed to know more about the Shop—to visit it, to smell the aroma, and to talk with the shop owner. Now I get to! In *Apparent Faith*, Karl took us through his journey of discovering a new perspective of God through parenting. In *The Tea Shop*, Karl takes us back to the Tea Shop to discuss how his changed perspective of God impacted his faith and to challenge us. How does a change in perspective about God's nature and character affect our every-day lives? Our faith practice? Our relationships? Our communities? Sit back, brew a cup of tea, and enjoy this vacation to the Tea Shop."

BEAU HOFFMAN, ESQ., CULTIVATOR OF
LOVE, FATHER, AND HUSBAND

"My current 'favorite' word is Curious. I am living in a place of exploring everything that is curious to me. One of those things, is exactly what I felt like Karl experienced in *The Tea Shop*. I love that Karl allowed himself to be curious to the experience, and then take it to the next level by actually allowing the experience to change him… to allow himself to evolve even more. I want to be the man with no name from the tea shop... I want everyone to be curious and look for the man with no name. Everyone deserves the chance to be changed by a simple act of love."

CHRISTINA JONAS, EXPLORER

"In an easy and short read, *The Tea Shop* is the story of a man's awakening to the realities that life is far more nuanced and complicated than we've been told, and that there is truth and love to be found in the most random, unexpected places."

DALLAS VERITY, PODCASTER

"So much about spirituality is simply learning to pay attention and see what's going on beneath the surface. Karl does this beautifully as he works through his pivotal experience in *The Tea Shop*. This book will inspire you to pay more attention in your own life and see the subtle but profound ways God is speaking to all of us."

BEN DELONG, AUTHOR OF *THERE'S A GOD IN MY CLOSET*

"Just as we can extract vital nutrients from tea leaves and thoroughly enjoy the satisfaction of a soothing cup of tea, Karl reveals spiritual, emotional, and relational wisdom from everyday experiences that provide sustenance to the soul. *The Tea Shop* is an enjoyable example of his skill and a delightful read indeed!"

MARK KARRIS, AUTHOR OF *RELIGIOUS REFUGEES: (DE)CONSTRUCTING TOWARD SPIRITUAL AND EMOTIONAL HEALING*

"Change is difficult for many of us. Karl shows that he's not afraid to change as he takes time to appreciate and understand new things. There is so much to learn, discover and explore. The Tea Shop is an amazing experience and journey told through the eyes and understanding of a contemplative."

KYLE BUTLER, INSPIRATIONAL MOTIVATOR

First Edition

Cover design and layout by Rafael Polendo (polendo.net)

ISBN 978-1-938480-68-3

This volume is printed on acid free paper and meets ANSI Z39.48 standards.

Printed in the United States of America

Published by Quoir
Oak Glen, California

www.quoir.com

茶莊

The
TEA SHOP

Karl Forehand

KARL FOREHAND

Table of Contents

前言

Preface

"Every day God invites us on the same kind of adventure. It's not a trip where He sends us a rigid itinerary, He simply invites us. God asks what it is He's made us to love, what it is that captures our attention, what feeds that deep indescribable need of our souls to experience the richness of the world He made. And then, leaning over us, He whispers, 'Let's go do that together.'"

BOB GOFF

THE PART THAT I PLANNED

This past summer, we went to visit my son in Taiwan where he teaches English. This was my second trip and this time we scheduled some time to go to the Southern section of the island. It is less densely populated and offered us the promise of an adventure. I was hungry for getting off the main path and experiencing the beauty of Taiwan. Possibly, I was trying to learn to express this part of my inner child. I wanted to have fun—I wanted to celebrate—I wanted adventure.

We had just participated in an intensive weekend where I discovered that I am at heart playful and adventurous. I thought, *Good, we are going to Taiwan and we can have some adventures there*. I imagined all the different things we might do even though I had very little knowledge of the South side of the island. On my first journey to Taiwan, I spent time with my son and our friends in Zhongli, then I went to visit a missionary in Taipei. I remember a lot of walking and eating. I tasted a lot of interesting food and met some really nice people. I got a foot massage (which was amazing) and did some pottery—mostly civilized "city" stuff. But this time I wanted to do something daring while spending time with my son and beautiful wife. Thoughts of getting lost on a mountain, finding a new experience away from the tourist maps or becoming immersed in the beautiful nature all around us intrigued me.

Part of that journey involved renting scooters to explore the stunning view of nature around Taroko Gorge National Park. As we were getting comfortable with our scooters to go to the Gorge, I suddenly found myself airborne. Instead of stopping smoothly at a stoplight, I was headed for the pavement just beyond the front of my rented scooter. I still have the scars from the places that contacted the Taiwan street. I'm sure Matt Damon or Jason Statham would have executed a slick roll maneuver and come away unscathed, but I gave up my precision stunt man moves in my 30's. I wasn't badly injured; however, it threw us for a loop that day. We had to re-plan our trip and I was convinced I had ruined the whole adventure.

Wave after wave of shame and disappointment washed over me; in addition to the pain and inconvenience of having to dress wounds for the rest of the trip and the inconvenience of paying for a broken scooter, I felt kind of foolish for wanting to have an adventure. Why couldn't I have just admitted that I'm a little old to be running around on scooters and looking for adventure when we could have just as easily been sitting on a beach watching the waves roll in? Those are the kinds of thoughts you think when you are sitting in a Taiwan clinic in pain from an accident and the immediate future is in question.

In that moment of my uncertainty, my son became like a father to me. He is a strong, capable man. When I was injured, he successfully found us a clinic on the South end of the island to get me some very capable, inexpensive treatment for my wounds. He communicated with the Mandarin speaking Taiwanese doctors and nurses where I had no idea what to say and even comforted me in my distress. He played the part of the father for me when I felt helpless—the son fathering his father—wasn't this supposed to happen late in life? The part that I orchestrated left me feeling like a child. So, I am grateful for my son—my best friend, who in my vulnerability, was strong for me.

THE PART I DIDN'T PLAN

My accident caused us to have a couple of extra days in the more populated Northern region. One night, as our host Tanya was dropping us off at the hotel after supper, Laura decided to ask, "Where can we pick up a teapot?" We were looking for a souvenir to bring back to our daughters to commemorate the visit but had been unable to take the time to do so yet. I had been a little too busy trying to turn this vacation around after I lost control of the itinerary.

Tanya told us to jump in her vehicle and we headed off into the night.

The streets normally were crowded full of scooters and pedestrians during the day. The scooters were like a swarm of bees that surrounded the never-ending stream of cars. People trudged along the busy sidewalks and carefully navigated the narrow and awkward terrain. But at night, everything was a bit slower and much less chaotic. As we stepped back into Tanya's suburban, it was almost like slowly being able to breathe again. By now, we trusted her to get us there safely and there were way less obstacles at night.

"This is it," she said.

We pulled up in front of what looked to me like a normal shop from the outside, approximately 12 feet deep and fifty feet long, this was not where I expected to find the teapot to take home to my daughters commemorating our trip. As with most of the time so far—this was not what I had imagined.

As Laura and I walked through the front door of the Tea Shop, I went into consumer mode. Being slightly uncomfortable, I zeroed in on our mission: the teapots. I remember a thick large slice of a tree as the focal point to the room—this tea table was common to many shops in the area. The table was heavily varnished but mostly covered with various trinkets and random items with barely enough room to place the tea pots. The shelves were packed with ordinary and exotic tea pots adorned with Chinese characters. There were also religious figurines and antiques and incense holders. It was almost like a second-hand store, but I got the impression that every article was important somehow. Outside the reach of my control and carefully constructed plans, I was about to experience something unforgettable. As Brené Brown says in her book *Daring Greatly*, "perfectionism is not the path that leads us to our gifts and our sense of purpose; it's the hazardous detours."[1]

It soon became apparent that the owner of this eclectic shop was the center of attention, several locals were gathered around and focused on him. He wore very modern clothes—a pair of slacks and a pullover shirt and a comfortable pair of shoes that

---

1 https://www.goodreads.com/quotes/6467312-in-fact-what-i-ve-heard-over-and-over-throughout-the

made a full day of standing tolerable. Though his weathered face showed some signs of his actual age, his body was like that of a young man. He moved with ease and later demonstrated just how agile and flexible he was. Tonya told us about his life which began as an orphan. His story was inspiring, although he did not seem to be living in the past.

Tanya introduced us and told those in the shop that we were looking for a teapot—At least that's what I think she told him. I actually don't know what was said because they were speaking Mandarin, probably in the Taiwanese dialect. I had tried to learn some of the language, but I failed miserably. To my delight, most of the locals wanted to practice their English with me anyways.

We were busily looking for a teapot and my eyes quickly were glazing over from the sheer amount of merchandise in the tiny space. The shop owner and the locals got a feel for what we were interested in and found several others that matched what we picked out. After we settled on a couple of teapots we were interested in, the man behind the table invited us to have tea with him. Even having given up caffeine a couple of years ago, I sensed this was going to be an experience—so, I agreed. Laura and I sat down with our son, Jordan, and our host Tanya to have a cup of tea.

The last time I had tea in a shop, I ordered from a cashier in a green apron who asked if I wanted sweetener and whether I wanted it cold or hot. After placing my order, I waited impatiently for two-and-a-half minutes while my drink was made to order. Taiwan is a little different. I sat directly across from the unnamed man in the mysterious Tea Shop. Having tea for some cultures is more of a ceremony or a process than just preparing a drink for a guest. He had a specific ritual that seemed to be a combination of precision and artistic flow. I would later discover this was his manner in most things that he did. Once the process begins, I discovered it just continues until something else happens to shift the focus. He would heat the water in some sort of modern contraption and then pour it over tea leaves in the tiny decorated pot. The individual teas seemed to have significance and required some approval and feedback. I was out of my element, so I generally just nodded and looked to Tanya for help.

I always describe the smell of Taiwan as unique, sort of like walking into my grandma's house when I hadn't been there in a while. It's not a good or bad smell—it's just the Taiwan scent. Yet, when in the Tea Shop, the tea seemed to overcome all other aromas and it made us feel something slightly different. I felt a peace and tranquility, which made me only a little bit uneasy.

Along with the constant supply of tea, the man began to share his practice. Tanya told us that he was telling us about his specific yoga practice that he learned from someone else. He demonstrated it by standing on a stool and showing us how flexible and agile he was. He felt it contributed to his youth and flexibility. It seemed to require an "ooh" and an "ahh" from me, so I obliged.

He was 60 years old but seemed to have the dexterity of a much younger man. As my envy grew, I desperately wanted him to give me a book or DVD about this practice. I was searching for things that would make my life work better. I didn't know all that I would take home from this shop, but I was sensing it was something good!

THE PART THAT GOT
BETTER

Several years previous, Laura and I had begun a journey of eating plant-based foods. What initially was motivated by health became motivated by values and ethics. When my son and Tanya told the man that we were plant-based, he promptly invited us to share his supper with him. I thought, *Ha! This is what usually happens when I go to the store—we watch a guy tell stories and then eat dinner with him!* Briefly, I wondered if this would be the part of the story where the Americans were all poisoned and the Taiwanese lived happily ever after. But I trusted Tanya and we agreed even though it was late, and we had already eaten, we would continue with our engaging host (the tofu was delicious and just another eclectic part of this experience).

As we finished dinner, Tanya helped negotiate a price for the teapots. She assured us it was a bargain. After that, without announcement, he immediately began to macramé a little twine rope braid onto the teapots. It was a connector from the handle to the lid to keep it from getting lost. As he did this, he would occasionally spring up, then dart to some area of the shop and return with something in his hand. He moved effortlessly like a teenager full of life and excitement and it made us feel special.

Though we were already full from supper, our generous host brought us peanuts and sunflower seeds. I was starting to feel a sense of connection with him and a satisfaction with making the decision to venture out into the night. This was an adventure I was going to be glad that I embarked upon.

Next, he arrived with a bottle. Something that the shop owner's friend said made me think this was a special deal. The enthusiastic tone of his voice seemed to exclaim, "That's a new bottle!" Tanya quickly explained that this was alcohol not usually given to foreigners. The label was colorful with Chinese characters, the liquid clear. It certainly seemed unmenacing on the surface. The thought quickly raced through my mind about dying right there in the Tea Shop from alcohol poisoning. My God, what would Laura tell the police? "Officer! My husband was poisoned by an uncommonly flexible yogi with no name who makes tea curated from the fountain of youth!"

The bottle looked like it held grain alcohol. If you have ever had moonshine—that's about the size of it. *Holy rice wine Batman!!!* That was strong stuff! Someone mentioned something about taste, but I couldn't feel anything in my mouth. I noticed he was beginning to fiddle with something else. This time it was his characters. Characters are how Taiwanese communicate visually. They are complex and usually depict a word or phrase instead of just one letter.

He gave us some business cards, then a sheet of graph paper with some characters he had written. Even Tonya was not much help understanding this writing. Although she is very wise and culturally literate, she said something like "I understand it, but it's very hard to explain." When he saw that we appreciated the characters, he began writing something for me. By this time, I was simply just feeling very touched. He seemed compelled to make me happy—whatever it took. This was beyond customer service—I think he genuinely wanted to make people feel joy. I don't know if he was focusing his attention on me, but it felt like it.

THE PART I WILL NEVER FORGET

The shop owner was one of those people that others are attracted to, but I experienced him as one of the most genuine people I have encountered in a long time. He had time for me, he was interested in me and he took the time to make me happy! Sure, the cynical consumer in me wanted to imagine that he was trying to take advantage of us. But he already had our money, and there was a delight in his eyes that could not be ignored. A sincerity if you will.

This book is a compilation of what I learned from this man I will never forget. Stunned, I walked out of the Tea Shop saying to Laura, *What just happened?* I have been thinking about our experience at the Tea Shop ever since. I was hoping for an adventure and astonished that I found it in a tiny little Tea Shop and in an unassuming man that couldn't even speak my language.

I hope that I can learn to slow down and be the kind of person that I witnessed that night. To be present with people and share my food with them, to take time to love people instead of just serving myself. Maybe I will remember to say something kind to the people I interact with when I buy and sell things.

I imagine Jesus to be a lot like the man with no name. Even though this gentleman probably wasn't a Christian, I was able to see Christ in Him. I cannot wait to go back to Taiwan and visit the nameless man in the Tea Shop. In the meantime, I'm hoping to bring the teashop to you in this book. This is his story as much as mine.

癒見茶莊

Unexpected Lessons
from the Tea Shop

INTO THE MYSTIC

"In the days ahead, you will either be a mystic or nothing at all."

KARL RAHNER

I think everyone has a basket where the words we don't quite understand all get discarded to. I had put words like magical, mystical, and paradox into the basket of unacceptable uncertainty. They were considered a waste of time because they ate away at my assurance that I was right and comfortable with my beliefs. Walking into the Tea Shop challenged me to reconsider my basket of unacceptable words. In Taiwan there were unknown religious symbols, unfamiliar dialects and customs, and traditions I had never experienced before. All of this seemed magical and mysterious and maybe even mystical—whatever that was. For once, I didn't try to understand it before I experienced it! I just walked in and left my basket on the sidewalk outside.

Recently, I have discovered the music of Van Morrison. *Where have you been all my life?* Most people my age that like Morrison probably discovered him decades ago, but I like to think he came along just at the right time for me. I love his song titled "Into the Mystic." I have learned with most music not to spend too much time trying to interpret every song. Most artists leave some type of mystery to their art and that is what makes it intriguing and interesting and worth the time to contemplate. "Into the Mystic" just sends my mind off away from the temporal and causes me to think a little more deeply.

The Evangelical tradition I was once a part of didn't talk much about the mystical even though the simplest definition of mysticism could be "Experiencing God" (there's even a book by that title!). I once heard it said that the author was a bit of a mystic, ironic given the context at the time. But what does *mystic* really mean? Some of this is a little confusing for someone with my background. Sure, I'd like to go deeper—I've personally instituted some practices like centering prayer, yoga and meditation. But what is this mysticism that people talk about?

I had the privilege to listen to Dr. Glenn Young, from Rockhurst University speak about this topic. I've come to realize that I know only a little about a lot of things. Dr. Young has spent his career primarily studying Mystical Spirituality. He spoke for 3 hours without notes. I am only all the more engaged when I feel someone's passion as they speak. I find that when people can study something their whole adult life, they tend to be less argumentative, more open and more excited about conversation. My hope for the world is to have more conversations about the things that matter. Possibly, we need more mystics.

Dr. Young confirmed the basic premise of mysticism—that it is a direct encounter with God. In contrast to our usual fascination with doctrinal logic, mysticism is experiencing directly the presence of God. During the Reformation, there seemed to be those that discouraged basing anything on experience. As a result, many of us have opted for an intellectual reading of Scripture and a dogged commitment to the written Word while we diminish any experiential interaction that cannot be verified in writing. Inversely, there are times where the pendulum has gone the other way and we are irresponsible with our experiences. I see people who are driven by past trauma that interpret through their reaction to the pain they feel inside. They are usually experiencing and responding to past trauma instead of current encounters with God.

Why then do we have these experiences? Maybe an important distinction to make is that experience is more than just feeling something—it's not just an emotion—it is an encounter. Also, mysticism is not just something that happens. We do not generally just stumble into it. It is a part of a spiritual practice. Dr. Young defines mysticism in this way:

"Mysticism is that part of Christian belief and practice that concerns preparation for, consciousness of, and effects from the direct presence of God."

Our practices not only help form us, but they also lead us to the place where we can have that direct encounter with God. There is some preparation involved.

Consider the actual experience of the direct encounter with the Divine. There are several different areas where mysticism might take place, but I don't want to define those for you. My primary takeaway from these sessions was that although mysticism may involve some solitude, it is also a part of the mainstream of our spiritual life. Dr. Young and I had an in-depth discussion about how Mary and Martha of the Bible represent contemplation and action. While we could argue that Jesus said one was more important than the other, many other passages tell us that Jesus was highly interested in His *ethos* (His practice), which involved not just going to the garden, but also coming away from there to exercise that practice.

The final part of mysticism is what Bernard McGinn simply called the "effects" of the encounter. The result of the encounter with the Divine is that we move from that sacred space and express to others what God has impressed upon us. When we experience the love and adoration of the Divine, we become different. It doesn't just affect us, but it has an effect on others.

I lean towards the interpretation that Van Morrison's song was a love song of sorts. He was sailing home to see his love. But isn't that what we long for when we consider mystical things? We long to be home with the one we love. We long to feel the sweet embrace. We long to have deep conversations and savor our time together. When we imagine traveling "into the mystic," we should not be afraid. It is somewhat like a love song, but maybe even something deeper. It is more like a face-to-face, direct encounter where all the coverings and facades are removed.

The Tea Shop was my introduction into the mystical. Not because it was mysterious, but because it was so real. I left the Tea Shop believing that I had experienced God face-to-face even though the man with no name might have believed completely different from me. The subject of our religious beliefs never came up, even in translation, but the experience of God was as real as anything I have ever experienced.

Maybe it's because God is experienced most vividly in relationship. We were created from relationship and for relationships. Whether we are comparing a Baptist to a Methodist or a Catholic to a Buddhist, all of us draw lines of distinction where we think God cannot speak. To paraphrase Richard Rohr, truth is truth no matter where it comes from and God's love knows no boundaries and doesn't wait for us to come into agreement before He starts to work. God was, without a doubt, at work in the Tea Shop.

I describe myself as mystical, probably because I'm way more interested in those things than I used to be. Part of my journey is to put language to the things I'm discovering, but I hope the other part of my journey is mystery and paradox and the actual encounters that I sometimes can't even describe. Some of the best things about being married only get muddied when you try to define them. Love songs are really poets trying to put into words what cannot be adequately defined. So, I hope my mystical experiences have more of an outward flow that benefits me and the people I encounter. As the song alludes to and as I experienced in the Tea Shop, let us "float into the mystic."

SELF-GIVING LOVE

"...many of us still believe that the center and source of all existence is a self-giving, other-centered love. Here there is no hierarchy of power, no hierarchy of value and no hierarchy of respect." [1]

WM. PAUL YOUNG

All of us make assumptions. Even in stating this I'm assuming something about you, the reader. Most of these assumptions are based on our beliefs which for many are just assumptions about what is true. I was raised to assume things are a certain way and that certain rules apply. Beliefs are sometimes based on experience—if something behaved a certain way before, we assume it will behave that way in the future.

I think one of our basic assumptions is where we will find love. We assume that we will find love in places like church, that we will experience love at home, and we expect to feel love from family but certainly not from a stranger. I assume that people who are like me will love me and those that are different from me are somehow the enemy or just not that interested in me. All of these are assumptions; judgements that we make about ourselves or others. But, what if these assumptions wrong?

Upon entering the Tea Shop, I admit I carried with me a whole list of assumptions. I could trace many of these back into my checkered past of beliefs and biases that were built from my experiences, learnings, etc. However, the Tea Shop experience shattered many of the assumptions I had and continues to challenge them even now.

First, I assumed that buying an item from a retail store was simply transactional, not relational. In stores like Wal-Mart, I learned it is possible to avoid all human contact with store employees if you can dodge the greeter at the door. There are huge signs that point to the right department, and a complex description of the products on the boxes that house the product. If that doesn't work, we can google it and find even more information about what we want to purchase, even seeing reviews from others. We take the items to purchase to the front of the store, and thanks to more advances in modern technology we can now further avoid human contact through "self-checkouts." We have developed the habit of completing the transaction and ignoring the relational part of shopping. In some ways, this appeals to the typical male—get in, find what we are looking for, pay, and get out.

Second, I assumed that shopping should be efficient. Since Henry Ford developed the assembly line in the U.S., many of us have been on a quest to become more efficient. We even tried this with our food which has led to increased heart disease, high blood pressure and diabetes. I love to make the processes in my life more efficient. From walking the dog to cooking my supper, if I can save money, save time or make it better, I'm all in. As a result, I am constantly looking for ways to make things better. Efficient—*maybe?* But I'm not sure if it is good or bad. Efficiency was just one more assumption I carried with me into the Tea Shop.

Third, I assumed a whole rolodex of labels including "heathen." My past tradition used this to define anyone that wasn't converted to believe our particular doctrines. The assumption is that those who are different from us are somehow inferior to us. Whatever I know and understand, they are "other" and so they must be a different class of human—more animal-like or savage. This process of demoting and re-classifying things other than us has gone on as long as humans have existed. We see this used everywhere from the Bible to how the U.S. described the Native Americans, we used similar language for African slaves, and now this kind of language is being used to label immigrants.

Even people in the Bible, tried to classify other nations as something other than themselves to justify wars, genocide, and the like. They even blamed it on God. Leaders like Hitler classified Jews as subhuman and convinced Catholic and Protestant believers to exterminate those other than themselves.

These classification and labeling practices continue to this day. A quick scan of the daily news shows us who to disregard, hate, or fear—all based mostly on hasty assumptions. When I entered the Tea Shop, I was growing to love the Taiwanese people, but those I did not know were still suspect. I did not want to hurt them, but I also didn't want to be caught in a dark

Tawainese alley by myself either. My cross-cultural experience in the Tea Shop revealed my prejudice about things I didn't fully understand. I didn't want to feel it—but I did!

Finally, I carried with me religious assumptions. My background taught me I had the answers and I needed to share this knowledge with others to save them. I knew that if I was a good Christian, then I should be trying to convince people that they were wrong (most religions label them as "lost") and I am right (labeled "saved"). Every day this happens but I think if I am honest with myself, it hasn't produced a good result. "I am right" and "you are wrong" are both prideful and judgmental statements.

Some readers of this manuscript may wonder, "But if it's truth, does it really matter if we are judgmental?" My former tradition subtly encouraged me to judge others because we believed we had the truth. For me, this wall of contradiction began to crumble when I considered a thought in my previous book, *Apparent Faith*. When someone proposed the hypothesis, "None of us is right," I began to ask the question, "What if I am wrong?" When I carry this question with me, I seem to get better results from my explorations.

My assumption was that these people could not possibly find the right path without me. I am thankful that this assumption was steadily eroding for over a year at that point in my life. My previous assumptions were starting to crumble, and this was probably the reason that my visit was so fruitful. I didn't feel the need to change the man with no name and he didn't feel the need to change me. We just kind of loved each other, which Jesus seemed to think was the most important thing to do.

For love to happen, we must switch the focus from transactional to relational. When I entered the Tea Shop, I experienced people focus their attention on me. The transaction of buying the tea pots took a couple of minutes, but the relational part of the visit took close to two hours. In Taiwan instead of greeting you with "How are You?" or "How are you doing?", they ask "Have you eaten?" Now, I am a cook and I'll admit that I often badger people to eat when they are at my house—it makes sense to me to meet their basic need for food by asking, "Have you eaten?" Transactional thinking leads to efficiency and serving the most customers. Relational thinking centers on love for other humans and pays a different kind of reward. I wasn't expecting the Tea Shop owner to teach me this, but he did!

I found it's easy to believe that God's love is relational as I have experienced love within the body of Christ. I learned about love from the sacrifices of people I know and from those I have had the privilege to love. According to Wm. Paul Young, this type of love is defined as love that is "other-centered" and "self-giving." I have experienced this type of love inside the church, but I have also found love's ugly cousins hiding there as well— self-centered love, selfish love, manipulative love. Maybe these types of love are not really love at all or maybe they were just polluted. Either way, what I experienced in the Tea Shop was a love that was other-centered and self-giving—this made all the difference to me.

For the people in the Tea Shop to love me, they had to value me. They sought out ways to make me happy, they were friendly to me and gave up two hours of their time to invest in me. They were other-centered and self-giving—they were lovers. Classifying someone as *other* only helps justify abuse of that other. Demoting other people doesn't help us to love them, it never makes the world better, and it never makes us righteous or holy or productive. The owner of the Tea Shop saw me as a fellow human being—he valued me—and, in turn, I learned to do the same.

Since I spent time in the Tea Shop on the other side of the world, I have attempted to translate these values into actions. I am trying to practice other-centered, self-giving love toward my wife and family. It is easy to assess what we can gain from relationships but much harder to imagine what we can give.

I hope to take this experiment a bit further and employ what Jesus called "loving our enemies." It is exciting when people who I didn't expect to love me show affection toward me, it teaches me something about myself and about God. But, what about the people that I know don't like me? What about the people that see me as sub-human? I hope I can fight the urge to retaliate or get them first by simply giving of myself whether it looks promising or not. Someday, maybe, I can ask the man with no name about this, but what I suspect is that this idea is one of those that will change the world. Jesus certainly seemed to think that it would.

In the Tea Shop, it was just overwhelming to literally feel the concern that these people had for us. I believe that focus and concern begin with the questions we ask. We need to ask the right questions. Do we ask what we can get from an encounter or what we can give? True giving is without expectation, less transactional and more relational. Do we ask, "How is this person like me?" or "How is this person different than me?" Looking for common ground builds relationships while looking for differences builds division and resentment. Do we ask what can I give to this relationship or what can I get from this interaction? One of these creates an atmosphere of poverty; the other works from our abundance.

The nature of the adventure is that we often find something different than what we were looking for. My excursion into a different culture, outside of my plans, caused me to consider something else that is connected to other-centered love.

I used to watch a lot of detective shows. You know the ones—the detective paces the interrogation room to intimidate the perpetrator and finally the detective gets frustrated and pounds the table yelling, "I want answers!" I often feel like the frustrated detective as I try to be a good parent and husband, even a good Christian. The Tea Shop taught me to focus on the questions. The answers will come later.

I am becoming more comfortable with uncertainty. I am learning to find as much joy in asking the question as in finding an answer. For example, "What if I am wrong?" As I do this, I realize I can only really find answers when I keep asking questions. Some answers come quickly while other answers can take years or decades to unravel—some questions may never have answers. But, still, I'm learning to ask good questions and I'm learning to be at ease when the answers don't come when I want them to.

Early in my life, I learned to set goals and revel in their achievement—to set expectations high and then meet them. As I achieved bigger and better goals, I applied this to my relationships and my religion. In a sense, I stopped asking questions and expected what I already knew to be realized. The Tea Shop shattered all of that—the owner didn't seem to have any expectations for me. I didn't need to help him meet some goal he had arbitrarily set. He sold me a dragon statue, but only after determining that Laura and I were born in the year of the dragon. He learned this about me and then matched an offering to me and not his desire for me. It was relational, and it made me happy.

I expect to find love in the Church and sometimes, I do. Certainly, that is where I learned about love and learned how to love, but church experiences have also hurt me as I often found something that masqueraded as love but really had the opposite effect. I learned about love from my family of origin. With all its challenges, my family growing up was a loving environment that helped shape me. The mistakes made in my family and the church were probably because we didn't know any better, so I try not to hold any grudges. My current family is where I find the most direct, Christlike love I have ever experienced. I would be devastated if I found that we no longer could love each other.

I went to Taiwan to have an adventure. I expected to find satisfaction by accomplishing my goals. Instead, I found love in a Tea Shop with a man who had no name. I wasn't even really looking for love, even though being loved/receiving love is one of the root cravings of the human soul. I am glad that I saw through my assumptions, stepped into a Tea Shop in Taiwan, and met the man with no name. He showed me a literal and physical example of other-centered, self-giving love and for this I am grateful.

ADVENTURES ARE UNSCRIPTED

"The big question is whether you are going to be able to say a hearty yes to your adventure."

JOSEPH CAMPBELL

I am part of a community of people who have experienced Breakthrough. Breakthrough is an immersive seminar that helps people address issues in their life. During the process, I developed a positive "I am…" statement based on the work I did there. My personal statement is: "I am a playful, adventurous, and mystical man who is enough." The playful part has to do with the celebration that I talked about in my previous book, *Apparent Faith*. The mystical part is because I want to have true experiences with God. The adventurous part is probably what led to the scooter ride and, ultimately, to the Tea Shop.

I have always gravitated toward adventure. I remember long summer days with one of my brothers, Monty—we discovered a creek that had crawdads, also known as crayfish, in it. We spent the better part of the morning searching under rocks for the elusive crayfish. If you have never seen one, they look a little like a tiny lobster. Early in the afternoon, we ventured to the other side of town on our bicycles to sell the crawdads to a bait shop we knew about. Could this be the dawning of a burgeoning empire? Probably not, since most of them died on the way to the shop. Oh well—on to another adventure! We spent the better part of one summer building a raft which we hoped to float in a nearby pond. We discovered that the pond was only about a foot deep when the raft sank in it. We just left it there.

Later in life as I became more successful, I missed most of the little adventures that came my way. I had forgotten that adventures did not necessarily have a specific outcome in mind, they were more a moving target that we adjusted as we searched for resources and found our way toward our ever-changing desires. One day, Monty and I had just decided to paint addresses on curbs, but after spending all our earnings on Dr. Pepper at the store we moved on to another adventure and changed the goal posts.

The business world taught me to have well-constructed plans. Brainstorming, focusing, goal setting, planning, resourcing, prioritizing, execution, evaluation. Wait, what about the new methodology? How can we implement these new strategies as we move forward? Just a few more meetings and we will be able to sell this idea and implement it before the end of the year. Corporate strategies are a little like adventures and that is probably why some people stay interested past the two-hour meeting. I imagine the great innovators and inventors and people that really changed our times were probably just kids that did not fully grow up and never really lost their sense of adventure. The rest of us are just trying to mimic what they did in a more organized and sometimes unproductive manner.

The original Taiwan-adventure was well-planned... that was my fault. I pushed my son (who is still comfortable with adventure) to put some definite plans in place so we would know what we were doing when we got there. It gave me a sense of peace to be able to have an itinerary when we were in a foreign country halfway around the world. It gave me some assurance to strategize and forecast, but I often wondered: How much preparation does it take to obliterate the true nature of an adventure? Is it an adventure if it is structured and planned and predictable? *Wait... do we need to have another meeting before we leave?*

Luckily, unexpected things happened that turned my well thought out planned excursion back into an adventure. Taiwan is well equipped with several trains that mostly run North and South the length of the island. One of them is the high-speed rail. Some of them have reserved seats and some of them are a kind of general admission. All are clean, inexpensive, and the people are mostly friendly. We were waiting for the train we were supposed to take when my son made a calculated move and said, "Hey, we could probably get on that train." *Ehhh, I don't know if that's a smart move*, I thought but I kept quiet because adventure sometimes means taking a little risk.

Jordan explained that the train we were on had reserved seats and our tickets were for the other general admission train..." but, it should be fine, there aren't that many people." I should admit that my wife, Laura, prefers not to break the rules. She's not against adventure, but she likes to follow the rules along the way. I know, it is somewhat of a contradiction, but who am I to tell her how to run her life? As we progressed South through the mountains, people began to board the train at each stop. Before we knew it, we were moving to different seats because people pointed at the seats and showed us their ticket—the calm Taiwan way of saying, "Get the heck out of my chair that I paid for!" Eventually, the reserved seats were all full and we were left standing in a passageway next to the bathrooms.

Before I go on, you *must* understand the bathrooms. They are exceptionally clean. The public restrooms are cleaned all day long. It made me a little uncomfortable. In the men's bathroom, it is not uncommon to see an older lady mopping the floor while dozens of men use the latrines. No yellow sign, no waiting for her to finish. Just a coexistence that seems normal to everyone, so I went with it. Some of the toilets are like the ones in the U.S., but some of them are more like a little bathtub on the floor. To use them, the best practice is to squat over them or else have good aim. I mention this because as we were standing in the passageway, I realized I was going to have to use one of these bathrooms and I was going to have to sit down (know what I mean?). Another adventure was just on the horizon for me.

Jordan coached me on the proper way to do this. I knew Laura would never go to this level of adventure, but me being the adventurous one (it's in my contract and all), I squatted down and tried to relax. I was having some success until the train rounded the bend (I assume) and began to kind of rhythmically slam me against the wall. You will be happy to know that everything was in its proper place and I accomplished my mission. Afterwards, I felt like just going to the bathroom was a good unexpected side adventure. Back home, the bathroom experience happens in a non-moving, even calm atmosphere. I would not label it adventurous. But even a tranquil restroom experience can turn into an adventure with the right conditions.

The conductor of the train finally caught up with us, insistent that we were on the wrong train. I think the cleaning guy snitched us out (maybe it had something to do with my little "mis" adventure previously mentioned?). Maybe he heard me carrying on in the bathroom, maybe he just hated Americans (might as well be paranoid, right?). After we paid the conductor the difference in price, he found us a nice seat up toward the front. I think Laura was embarrassed by the whole incident, but it reminded me of being a kid and running into an adult who finally had the courage to tell me to stop doing this or that which was out of the ordinary. I remember sliding down the escalator at the mall and having a similar outcome. Sometimes you have to color outside the lines a little by getting away from the master plan.

When we finally got off the train, we were going to walk to a hotel. The area was thick with travelers and some tourists from what I could tell. Immediately we were singled out by the cabbie who began talking us into staying at his motel. He spoke some broken English and seemed almost a little disappointed when Jordan could communicate in his native tongue. We kind of knew we were being scammed a little, but we were tired from the adventure and just wanted a place to stay. He drove us across town to the motel rooms above his house and we settled in for the night. It was cheap and clean and ultimately not that bad of a place. I was glad that I could dismiss the fact that this guy reminded me of several scary people in the movies.

I slept well, picked up some fruit at the market, and then we rented the scooters. After the scooter accident, we kind of stumbled around town, licked our wounds (so to speak) and attempted to devise a new plan. It seemed like the responsible thing to do. We still wanted to see Taroko Gorge National Park. Everyone said to go there, and our son had visited it previously with some of his friends. We discovered that we could take the bus to the gorge and then continue on foot. We would not see as much of the gorge, but maybe we could look a little closer?

That is exactly what happened. We spent most of the next day walking along trails toward the bottom of the gorge. We met some local indigenous people that sold us some trinkets and we did things like putting our feet in the water and exploring all the nooks and crannies of this magnificent landmark. As I put my feet in the water, my mind returned to that other adventure halfway across the world when we searched for crawdads. I almost started turning over rocks, but as I assessed our situation, I realized *we will never make it to the bait shop anyway.*

In summarizing the day, I felt thankful that plans had changed. The time spent exploring the gorge was the most memorable thing I had experienced so far. Beauty seemed to unravel all around me and even though it was uncomfortably hot, and I was exhausted, it was refreshing to know that something good came out of plans that did not come to fruition. I was beginning to understand what I knew as a kid. *Sometimes the best adventures are the ones that are unscripted.*

There are three types of adventure that speak to me: the things I sometimes plan successfully, the things that happen when plans change, and the things that just happen out of the blue. The things I can plan for and execute give me a sense of accomplishment. We need some order in our lives (thank you, Laura!), but not too much (thank you, Kids!). I need the unexpected changes, it brings color and variety to my grey and ordered day. The unexpected detours paint in the outline of my planning with a vibrant, watercolor splash of adventure. And then there are the things that we could never plan for and do not happen every day. For me, the Tea Shop was one such out-of-the blue experience. May I learn to experience those times and be grateful for what they teach me!

THE VALUE OF PRESENCE

"Do not dwell in the past, do not dream of the future,
concentrate the mind on the present moment."

BUDDHA

"Don't worry about tomorrow… Each day
has enough trouble of its own."

JESUS

I used to be a binge-watching fan of the hit TV series Dr. Who—don't judge, we've all done it. And do not ask me any specific questions because it was all a blur. I must have watched 50 or more episodes in the span of a week. It comes as no surprise then that most people are fascinated with traveling through time. We think *if we could just go back and fix this episode from the past* or *if we could go and see what the future is like* then everything would be alright in the here and now. As our mind takes the future trip or the past journey, we find ourselves absent from today. Often, Laura will say to me, "Are you here?" Every good film producer knows we like to time travel—every great philosopher and poet knows it is much better to stay present.

The Tea Shop was a great lesson for me in being present. It all happened so fast. I did not have time to plan anything, I couldn't plan what I was going to say, worry about how people would react, or generate a lot of expectations. One minute we were talking about teapots and the next minute we were there. That's the good thing about Tanya, our host. She doesn't allow for much discussion, she just reacts! It's as if she knows if we think about it too much, we will dredge up regrets from the past or trepidations about the future and won't move or fully enjoy the present. Five minutes after we asked her, "Is there a place to get tea pots?", we were standing in the doorway of the Tea Shop. We had no choice but to be present.

To be fair, there are probably a few times when it is valuable to time travel. Under the care of a counselor or a spiritual director, some time travel can do some good. Recently, I took a little journey to visit my past and was able to resolve some issues that affected the present. While the past is a good place to visit occasionally, we just can't live there. Journeying to the future can also pay some dividends if we use it to do some reasonable planning. The trouble of course is that we plan excessively without the ability to predict the future accurately or completely. We drive ourselves crazy sometimes with future "what if's?"

When I left the Tea Shop, I said out loud, "What happened?" I said the same thing the other night when Laura tricked me into clothes shopping. I did not have time to execute my normal battle plan. My normal strategy goes something like this:

Plan out the future event (like going to a Tea Shop), calculate all the obstacles, do a little research, think about what I will say in certain situations, and then make alternate plans of escape or avoidance of the unpleasant. But above all, be in charge of how this comes out—being in control is necessary for my survival! The guiding forces in my battle plan are the regrets of the past and the fears of the future. In this way, I avoid the uncertainty of the present by fighting the battles I am familiar with over and over to assure that I will always win.

As I entered the Tea Shop, I tried to contrive a hasty action plan. I thought to myself, *I've been in shops before: find what you like, get in, get out, and above all, get a good deal.* But the owner of the Tea Shop had a different plan. He stopped me, spoke to me and brought me back to the present. He told us about himself, gave us food and by his conversation and body language communicated he was genuinely interested in us. All of this snapped me out of recreating the past or avoiding the future. I became fully engrossed in being present with him. It brought a richness to the moment, colors seemed to be more vibrant, and the conversation clearer and more fruitful. No one was daydreaming in this classroom. We were all present.

In a movie, the dream sequence makes the present cloudy and brings into focus a different time or imagination. In life, time travel clouds the present. I am not fully experiencing what I can be when I am future tripping or past journeying. I am not really hearing my wife, I'm not really experiencing a situation, or I'm not truly living if I am not living in the now.

For those of you who are older, you will remember that at the beginning of every class in school the teacher took roll. I remember in fifth grade, Mrs. Beaty would call out each student's name and the student would respond with "here" or "present". However, being how I was, I'd call out in my fifth-grade voice, "President" instead of "present." To this day, I still hear her say, "Just say present, Mr. Forehand." For past-era teachers, "here" or "present" would work fine, but today most teachers would probably understand there is a difference between being just *here* versus being *present*. It is very easy for me to be here and not be present. If Laura (Did I mention she's a schoolteacher?) asks me if I'm here, what she really means is, "Are you present?"

The past couple of days, I have focused on being present no matter where I am. I recently had a job interview during which I felt like I was totally present. It was a good reminder of how I want to live my life. I fully understood what the guy was saying—we were in sync throughout the conversation. The hour passed quickly.

I am realizing, though, that it takes practice to stay present. I have spent a lot of years living the other way. Starting today, I am implementing a little strategy, so, as the reader, you are responsible to keep me accountable—my publisher assures me your contract for responsibility is in the small print on the book jacket. In every situation, I'm going to imagine Mrs. Beaty from fifth grade calling roll and under my breath I'll respond, "President," and I'll chuckle to myself and focus my attention on the situation I am in and not the places I tend to go.

Thank you Mrs. Beaty and Laura and the guy in the Tea Shop, for teaching me to be present!

DELIGHT

"This is my beloved son in whom I am well pleased."[2]

GOD

In the Tea Shop I experienced a wave of emotions, many of them took me a long time to decipher. I experienced satisfaction, a bit of fear, some good old-fashioned joy, and even some sadness when it was over. However, one emotion undergirded them all—"delight." The simplest definition of the verb *delight* is to "take pleasure" or "please greatly." At Jesus' baptism, God the Father said He was *well pleased* with Jesus. As far as I can tell, He wasn't saying that Jesus did something to earn His favor, it seems that His delight was simply something present on Jesus.

Other words for delight are charm, enchant, captivate, bewitch, thrill, excite and take someone's breath away. I experience these emotions every time I visit my grandchildren. Jackson and Hollyn charm, enchant, and captivate my attention every time I see them. As powerful as that is, I think delight is even more powerful when it comes from an unexpected source—like the Tea Shop owner. I was not expecting to experience a sense of delight when I walked into the Tea Shop. I expected a Wal-Mart experience as we were tired, frustrated, and honestly just wanted to make a quick purchase—get in, get out, and get back to the motel.

Some people love to delight in others. I am not talking about the actors of the world that try to charm people as eventually we see through them and their superficial act to win our favor and it comes across empty and void of heart-felt love. What I am talking about is an intention that is based out of love—a desire to see beauty in someone else. I experience this when I gather with others, see through all the messiness and chaos they bring, and still enjoy the moment. Somehow, these people are captivated and enchanted by simply being with other humans. It takes some determination, the right attitude, and living from our heart. I experienced delight-centered people in the Tea Shop and hope to develop this in myself.

The Father, Son and Spirit are in a relationship with each other, it was out of this relationship that the Father delighted in the Son (Jesus). Eugene Peterson describes this relationship in each other as *perichoresis*: "Imagine a folk dance, a round dance, with three partners in each set. The music starts up and the partners holding hands begin moving in a circle. The tempo increases, the partners move more swiftly swinging and twirling, embracing and releasing. But there is no confusion, every movement is cleanly coordinated in precise rhythms as each person maintains his or her own identity."[3] My grandchildren are in a relationship with me and I'm enchanted with them—not because they are perfect, but because we are in a relationship together. Delight is not automatic in those that we share relationships with, but it is easier to delight in those we know than those we do not. What I learned from the Tea Shop is that we can delight in those we barely know if we decide to. I did not decide that right away, but this man delighted in me as soon as he saw me. I am not sure exactly why, but you could see it all over his face. He took great pleasure in us and was thrilled to put his energy into that dance of delight.

Often, I find that I reject the idea that I could delight in those that are different from me. The Tea Shop taught me differently. We were from different cultures, we spoke different languages, we had different belief systems—but somehow, in the Tea Shop, I learned to delight in others. It may have been because of the differences that we were so charmed with each other. I am striving to remember this as I have opportunities for delight each day. If I can overcome my fears, then I can move toward the opportunities I have to be with others and delight in their presence.

Recently, I was with my friends who run Breakthrough, conducting a seminar that they have been doing for over 20 years. I was one of the rookies, helping with all sorts of details like setting up the chairs and interacting with the participants. Usually I think too much and sort of freeze up at these types of events. However, this time I decided to be present and simply delighted in the process. I allowed myself to hear what they were saying and see their body language that told me even more. I kept my mind from wondering too much and noticed details that I would not normally have seen. I was determined to allow myself to be captivated by the process and charmed by the participants and the leaders. As I write this it sounds scary, but it took my breath away because I was open to delight.

I think because we were created for and from a relationship, living from a heart of love, delight is the natural state for those in a relationship that allow it to happen.

MORE ABOUT LOVE

"If I speak with the tongues of men or of angels, but do not have love, I am only a resounding gong or a clanging cymbal."[4]

THE APOSTLE PAUL

Several years ago, I was officially categorized as a missionary. When I replanted a church in America, it was considered mission work, even though I was only driving less than an hour away. I admire missionaries and the work that they do. Being a missionary is kind of like being a teacher or a nurse. They never get paid in proportion to the job they do; they are often under-appreciated, and sometimes forgotten. I'm sure most missionaries with more experience would have known how to approach the people in the Tea Shop but my instincts are sometimes not that great. Whether I am in an unfamiliar town in the United States or in a foreign country, like Taiwan, I often don't approach things as well as I could. I seem to stress the wrong things or have the wrong attitude. I think to myself, *"If I could just find the right method... If I could make my speech more eloquent... If I could find the right argument... then I would be able to convince them or help them or... whatever it is that good missionaries do."*

A few days ago, I found a new profession for myself. I might just be a car salesman. I know, I know—even I did not imagine I would do that. I used to categorize car salesmen with lawyers—just another crook out to get my money. In my mind, car salesmen were just a level above politicians. But, of course, generalizations usually are not based on truth or data, just bad perceptions. I have a good friend that is a lawyer, and he's a really good guy. I think it is kind of like the assumptions people make about pastors. I began to imagine what my life would be like as a car salesman, solving people's car problems. I even started to go through all the conversations I would have in my mind and what I would say when people did not want what I was selling. But maybe, just like missionaries or pastors, always having the right thing to say is not what is most important.

The Apostle Paul seemed to think this way. In his letter to the Corinthians, he stressed that even if what is said is angelic, it is only going to sound like noisy gongs and clanging symbols to people if it's not said out of love. I had to let that soak in for a while when I read it this morning. *What is the most important thing I can say in any situation?* If what I say or do is not done in love, then what I say or do will come across wrong. Whether I am a car salesman or a missionary or a pastor, other-centered, self-giving love may be the secret weapon to life that we have missed.

As a Christ follower, it would be hard to argue that anything matters more than love. As Theodore Roosevelt once said, *people*

don't care how much you know until they know how much you care.[5]
Love is a fruit of the Spirit. It is the heart of the great commandments that Jesus talked about. All the eloquent approaches that we hope will manipulate people will only cause them to cover their ears unless the primary action is love.

In the Tea Shop, love looked like a man with no name sharing his tofu with me. Love was exhibited in his interesting smile and his energy for us and the time that he took to make us feel special. Love seemed to be common in the Taiwanese people. They generally and genuinely exhibit love toward others. I learned of this love from my family and my religious tradition. Unfortunately, sometimes I do not see this in people that profess the name of Christ. Maybe I just expect too much from *God's people*. Paul goes on to describe what this looks like.

> "Love is patient, love is kind. It does not envy, it does not boast, it is not proud." [6]

Could it be that we are too concerned with angelic speech and flawless, proven methods and we forgot that what matters more than anything is other-centered, self-giving love? Not just thinking loving thoughts, but doing loving things?

When we shop at Wal-Mart, we always take our own bags. We figure it is one of the small things we can do to help save the planet. We probably own 50 of these bags, because we keep forgetting them at home and we buy more. I think we might be defeating our own purpose there. Sometimes, using the bags causes distress at the checkout counter because they take a little longer to load and often the next person in line sighs a little because it takes slightly longer to get through the line.

We haven't been yelled at yet, but sometimes we catch an ugly stare. It says something about us that one or two extra minutes might just ruin our entire day. The people in the Tea Shop were not in a hurry, because real love is *patient*. They spent almost two hours showing us genuine love. They gave us their time and attention and even displayed in their attitude what I would call Christ-like love.

Sometimes the words we use can be confusing. For example, sometimes where I live, we can be very nice, but that doesn't mean we are necessarily being kind. Some call it "Midwest Nice." It's slightly different from the "bless your heart" in the South, but it has about the same effect. It does not really fool anyone, but it satisfies our desire to conform to our manners and social norms. It makes us feel better, but it is not really love. According to Paul, love is *kind*. Kindness is other-centered and self-giving. It's not just a proper word, it's the proper attitude. It's not just what's accepted, it's what is necessary. My friends from the Tea Shop were genuinely kind—we could see it in their eyes filled with grace, you could feel it in their healing actions, and we left feeling loved instead of feeling used.

In my last book, I examined the fact that my pastor thought I was evil at seven years old. He told me that I was so bad that God had turned his back on me. He didn't say this directly to me, just in the general invitation to the congregation. By process of elimination, I discovered that my main sin at the time was probably covetousness or *envy*. Why is envy wrong? Envy is wrong because it isn't thankful for what it has, and it isn't happy for what others have. It wants to rearrange everything to my advantage. It is something we learn early in life when we claim as "mine" something that doesn't belong to us. Love means genuinely learning to be happy for others without having to take what they have or be unsettled about it. For me, this lesson was reinforced by the Tea Shop owner because neither of us really wanted to be the other person or have what they had. Because we were so different, maybe those imaginations seemed to be distant and we were both just content being who we were. Possibly, it is a little easier to envy those that are more like me. For that brief time, I experienced contentment.

I admit that I have a little bit of an inferiority complex. I have a need to perform and find approval from others. This can lead to being boastful or prideful. I don't feel superior to others—I feel inferior and that is what leads me to drone on about what I am doing or what I have accomplished. If the people in the Tea Shop would have been able to speak my language, I might have introduced myself by boasting about what I do or what I have or what I have accomplished. But, because I could not speak their language, I had to focus on more basic, more loving, and less boastful communication. They also had the same dilemma and the result was a better interaction.

We tend to consider the base things as the lesser things. In the case of love, the basic thing is the most important thing. Paul says, without it we are "nothing." It is not only an important element, it is the key ingredient to living a productive, healthy, fruitful life. We cannot say we are followers of Christ and not love our neighbors and our enemies. It is incongruent and doesn't even make sense when reading His words.

As I look back over the first half of my life, I often regret the time that I spent foolishly. In my desire to make my life more efficient, I often bypassed opportunities to spend time with people and show them genuine love. From what I read about Jesus, he often spent time just being with others and showing them genuine compassion. What would have happened if I would have invested even 10 minutes every day in just showing kindness and love to one person? Thankfully, there are reminders along the road of life. Occasionally, I see models of this Christ-like behavior in the people I know. Sometimes I see it clearly in my wife and children. And then, every so often, a co-worker or friend surprises me with unconditional love. But, on that day in Taiwan, I saw it in the people gathered in the Tea Shop.

My aspiration as a car salesman, provided that is what I choose, is likely to be like the man with no name in the Tea Shop. Of course, they won't let me have food in the showroom and people don't like tofu all that much. But I hope that I can exhibit the kind of love I experienced halfway around the world no matter the job I am employed to do. I hope I can take my time with people and be patient. I hope I can listen to people's sacred stories without having to drone on about mine. I hope they experience love in what I have to say and don't hear me as a noisy gong or a clanging cymbal. Since I do like to eat, I hope to sell lots of cars; but then I remember the Tea Shop owners didn't have a problem with selling me what I wanted because they loved me first!

WHAT I DIDN'T DO

"It's not what I did, it's what I didn't do."

GEORGE JONES

How do I really feel about people? As long as I can remember, I have longed to understand how people work. I love to read about how we function biologically, socially, and emotionally. Maybe that is one of the reasons I became a pastor. Sometimes, this quest uncovers the ugly side of people and I make broad generalizations about them. Even though I don't intend to, I subconsciously classify people so that I can know how I feel about them as a group. Evaluating people as a group is way less time-consuming that treating them as individuals. This is unfortunate because what I believe about people influences how I treat them.

There was a time when I would have had at least some amount of racial misunderstanding. I call it a misunderstanding due to ignorance from an inheritance of some suboptimal beliefs. Over time, as I have experienced life, my patterns and beliefs have changed. It would be irresponsible to say I don't have any limiting beliefs in this area, but I think I am maturing.

This has led to discovering that I once held a belief of *exceptionalism*. Exceptionalism is defined as "a theory that a nation, region, or political system is exceptional and does not conform to the norm."[7] Another similar term is *triumphalism*, which is described as, "smug or boastful pride in the success or dominance of one's nation or ideology over others."[8] Many recent politicians have spoken about a "city on a hill," and, as a result, I often found myself able to justify my disdain for other people, cultures and nations because they were not *us*. These *others* were classified as the *enemy* because their beliefs were somehow inferior to my belief system and/or my nation, in my own opinion. This pattern of belief is not Christ-like in any way, but it has become common and even acceptable in American Evangelicalism.

In my previous book, *Apparent Faith*, I wrote about how my views on nationalism and violence have changed recently. I believe that below these higher-level beliefs must be something more core and basic: how do I really feel about people? Before I form my thoughts about war and race and violence and nationalism, I must go deeper. How do I feel about human beings that inhabit this planet? Genesis declares there is no exception to humans being made in the image of God. If I deserve life, liberty and the pursuit of happiness, then why don't all people deserve that? What makes me an exception? If all men are created equal, doesn't that apply to whoever I consider to be my enemy right now? What makes my enemy an exception?

I wouldn't consider myself someone who has negative feelings towards any nation or race or gender based on those identities alone, and even my religious disdain for other beliefs has been waning recently (now that's a miracle). However, I do consider myself to have some residue of an attitude of American triumphalism and exceptionalism. I may even admit to taking the "city on a hill" a little too far and imagining that the United States is a New Jerusalem instead of an empire like Babylon (Jesus originally talked about a "city on a hill" but the term now has little to do today with what He meant when He originally said it). I admit that I still had thoughts about convincing those people of my beliefs that were obviously at least superior to theirs before I visited Taiwan. I'm so glad that these prideful beliefs, all wrapped up in my ego and my fears, are beginning to slowly fade away.

I find myself much more able to be present with people when I am not trying to change them. When I do not see them as the other, I listen more effectively and find better ways to show love and compassion for them. I understand what people are saying more often because I accept them the way they are. It is so freeing not to have to run the world. In general, I am free to think what I want, but what I think about others changes everything.

For whatever reason, when I entered the Tea Shop, I was humbled enough by the scooter Incident to be present and experience all the good things that happened that night. Maybe it was my embarrassing wreck on the scooter or the jet lag or the interesting train ride through the mountains, all I know is that I was ready to savor this once-in-lifetime experience, not because me or my country was exceptional and not because they marveled at my "city on a hill," but because all of us were able to sit at the same table, break bread together and experience each other. For whatever reason, all the barriers were taken down and I was able to be present in the moment.

I long to see a world of people that imagine how they will treat each other before they consider how exceptional they are. This is my hope for the world and all religions, and it is my hope for my family and the other communities that I am involved with. This is what I hope for my new workplace and other places I visit every day. I long to see the Kingdom that Jesus talked about as He traveled the ancient countryside. Maybe, if I listen close enough, one day I will be able to hear the faint whisper of the words He spoke. Maybe, if I put aside my sense of nationalism, pride and religiosity and really hear his desire for the Church, I'll understand what He meant when He said:

But to you, who are listening I say: Love your enemies, do good to those who hate you, bless those who curse you, pray for those who mistreat you.[9]

As I listen to others, I am inclined to believe that Jesus' words in his day are gaining traction in our day. It is of course not without opposition, but if I can wander into a Tea Shop and put Jesus' words into action, then take my word for it, anyone can!

萍水相逢

The Rest of the Cast

THE HOST

Remember to welcome strangers in your homes.

HEBREWS 13:2

I can't imagine what a trip to Taiwan would be like without a host. Many of the people there speak English but visiting Taiwan would still be much more difficult without a host that was interested in making our trip better. My son met Tanya and Phil through the Taiwanese family that ran the restaurant where he worked during college. When he visited during the summer of his Senior year, Tanya and Phil hosted him and gave him a place to work, eventually they helped him find a permanent teaching job. When I went to visit, Tanya volunteered to be our Host and take care of us.

Tanya graduated from college in the states, so she spoke English very well. In Taiwan, her family owns a medical clinic and they developed an ointment that is somewhat famous. Having quick access to a medical clinic came in handy when I had the scooter accident. They patched me up and gave me supplies to take care of the wounds. You really have to be careful what you say around her though. When I said my back was a little sore, the next thing I know I'm having a conversation with Dr. Happy. Dr. Happy was named after his dog, Happy. I don't know how that works. The family also owns an American style restaurant. That comes in handy, although they have taken me to several "special" places every time I have been there, like the famous fish restaurant and the drive-in pancake shop.

Some of the experiences we had wouldn't have been possible without Tanya. When we mentioned we needed a Tea Pot at 10:00 p.m., she was able to take us directly to a shop and introduce us to the owner. Earlier in the trip, she took us to a famous fish restaurant, and we had lunch with the owner. We ate with some Korean tourists whom she was also hosting. For a person who runs two businesses to spend their waking moments planning and organizing events to make other people happy seemed very unusual to me. For instance, we were a little stressed out at one point during the trip. Tanya noticed and arranged for us to have a foot massage, she pulled into the business and ordered us inside. Now, Tanya is one of those people you just don't argue with; when you are riding in the car with her, you don't really ask questions, you just hang on tight and wait with anticipation until you pull up to the restaurant or shop or wherever she has determined you are going next. The good news is that it was always exciting, and I was surprised nearly everywhere we went with her.

Don't try to pay her back though, I learned my lesson about trying to pay her back the hard way. They tell me that Asian people don't like to be indebted to anyone. When I was out shopping on my first trip, I got her a gift to thank her for hosting me. When she saw it, she kind of hung her head because she felt like she owed me something now. She lightly scolded me since that was her job as host to do things for me. I didn't owe her anything. There is a lesson in there somewhere. The way she paid me back was to buy me some pineapple cakes, which are a traditional Taiwanese treat. She didn't however just give me a couple as we were out that day. She gave me a whole case of pineapple cakes hours before I left to come back to the States. She made sure she would not be indebted to me.

As I reflect on the Tea Shop experience, every aspect of it was due to Tanya making things happen. First, she got us there in record time. Did I mention that it is terrifying to ride with her? Next, everything she did was designed to help us succeed. She negotiated a good price for the teapots we bought. She also encouraged us to slow down and take the time to visit with the owner instead of rushing through it like we would usually be inclined. She is also the one who took pictures to preserve the moment. She was intensely interested in us getting the absolute most out of every experience.

I remember once when my mom came to visit, and I made her go on a food drive with me. My mom loves to work, so she kind of enjoyed it, but I realize now it violated the Wu code of conduct for hosting. When I went to see my brother in Colorado, he made me work for two days on his garage. He didn't force me, but I knew if we didn't do something like that, we would have been terribly bored. Like when he described his gun collection to me—he's very thorough. Tanya would have passed out if she saw a guest working.

I found out how serious the Wu family takes hosting when we went to a birthday party for her three triplet children. First, let me say, this was a party! There were costumes, lots of food, and a magician. Around 100 people, adults and children, were packed into this large upper floor of the restaurant. When the party was forming, I tried to help set up chairs and was quickly instructed not to help because I was the guest. So, I sat back and enjoyed the party, but when they started cleaning up, I started to pick up plates to throw them away. Tanya's mother would have nothing of it and seized my hand and very sternly said, "No, No!" I got the message: I was the guest and I was to relax.

My two trips to Taiwan have both been a whirlwind. Tanya always has a plan, but no one knows what it is because her one and only purpose, like the Tea Shop owner, is to make us happy. She scurries about planning and scheming and organizing on the fly to squeeze the most fun, food, and adventure into our trip. I am so thankful that we know her. Apart from my son, she is probably the main reason that I love Taiwan.

So, what's the point? I'm wondering what would happen if I lived my life more in this way. What if I could be more like Tanya and look for ways to make "other" people happy? What if, when I have some extra money, I would find someone that I could do something for? What if I didn't announce it to everybody when I did something nice? What if I did it just to see the smile on their face? I desperately want to learn how to do this. I think this is part of what Jesus had in mind when he said,

"Love your neighbor." I think it's what he demonstrated when he washed the disciple's feet and I hope when I start my new job that maybe, instead of looking for ways to make money, I can look for ways to serve others. I think those two things can complement each other, but we have to sow before we reap. I think all of us have something unique we can give, from the guy that gave me the foot massage to the person that made me a pancake as we were leaving Taiwan, we all can find ways to love others.

MY SON

"This is my beloved son, in whom I am well pleased."

GOD THE FATHER

I have always been able to relate to the "one and only son" reference in the Bible. Although my daughters have a very special
place in my heart, I only have one son and that makes it special
in a different way. He was also my firstborn, so there is that different dynamic with him as well. I love that we are best friends. I
firmly believe that parents must take on the role of a parent and,
in many ways, forget about being friends. But, if you are lucky,
after all the parenting is complete and the child leaves the house
an adult person, the friendship still survives. I am a lucky father
because our friendship has lasted into his adult years. I say I am
lucky, but I think we are friends because we both worked at it
very hard. We had all the struggles that every parent and child
had, but in the end, we found a way to respect each other—and
isn't that mostly what friendship is all about?

The best part about the Tea Shop adventure is that my best
friend was there. For this trip to Taiwan, Jordan (or J.D. as I

call him) sometimes played the part of the host, when Tanya wasn't there. But, as we visited the Tea Shop, he was my friend and experienced this with me. It wouldn't have been the same if he wasn't there. J.D. has always had the gift of being funny. I know a lot of people that think they are funny, but he is. On this night, he humbled himself because it was the shop owners time to shine. J.D. didn't take the role of a typical twenty-something and roll his eyes as if to say, "I'm not impressed." Rather he joined in with us and enjoyed the night alongside us. That meant so much to me. I think I'm a likeable guy, but I can't tell you how hard it is for me to get someone to go with me to a baseball game. I guess people generally do not think of me as someone to hang out with—but my best friend was there with me that night and I'm grateful for it.

If you think I'm bragging about my son, you are right! I really do not believe that I did anything outstanding to make this happen. I was not the perfect parent by any means and J.D. made a few mistakes along the way. What I am celebrating is that somehow, through all my mistakes, being a pastor's son, and all our ignorance as parents, he emerged as a fine human being. I know every parent says something like that, but really, I had the privilege of raising an outstanding man that has unique gifts and talents—and now, he is my friend.

When we made introductions at the Tea Shop, and always when I introduce my son, I think of the scene at Jesus' baptism when the Father says, "This is my beloved son, in whom I am well pleased." It really is less about what my son does and more about our relationship. Less about what we have in common than what we feel for each other. I can feel it when he hugs me. We genuinely long to see each other. Maybe it's the distance (he lives in Taiwan now) because there were seasons of our life as he was growing up that I wanted to strangle him. Now that he's all grown up, all I can think is, "I can't wait to see him again!"

People always hope that their children will respect them. We hope the body of work we put forward was enough to gain their respect, even though we know we made mistakes and, to be honest, we are usually hoping for a little grace and mercy. I think my children respect us for the most part, but what I am most proud of is the way they show respect for other people. In the Tea Shop, J.D. was extremely respectful of people that he didn't know. He is the same way about disenfranchised people and minorities and the less fortunate. He is a fairly pure example of love for all people with one exception.

If you are a person that abuses the less fortunate and uses politics and power to take advantage of others, then you're probably not on his friends list. He respects women, he respects older people, and he is kind to children and animals. He even is kind to the people in Taiwan that out him as a "foreigner." He was kind to the little girl that treated him like a freak because he had a big beard and a towel on his head. Forget that he is my son, I am so proud that I have a friend that is kind, generous and respectful to all human beings.

At the Tea Shop, J.D. said very little because it wasn't the right time, but I find I want to listen to him more and more. He has a writing outlet and a podcast. He and his friends are a little outspoken about politics, but they always bring up intelligent and thought-provoking ideas about the situation of the world, and especially about the United States. There is passion and concern in his voice, along with a rational line of thinking. It doesn't matter if I agree with every point he makes or not, I still want to say to my friends "Listen to him!" I think that is what the Father was saying about Jesus at the transfiguration. When Jesus was there with Moses and Elijah, the Father says to them and Peter, James and John, "Listen to Him!" He was stressing to them, "Get out of your mindless patterns and listen to these thoughts that he has about how to change the world—open up your mind—use your brain and consider some different options!" It's one of the proudest parts of being a parent when your children learn to think for themselves.

I am proud of my son. I probably imagined he would be a sports star, but I was ignorant. I probably imagined he would praise me more and feed my ego, but I was immature. What surprises me every day is that he calls me a friend—that he says, "Love you, Pops!" Those are the things that matter. The best thing about the Tea Shop, wasn't that any of us were impressive but that all of us were sharing the experience together.

MY WIFE

"You are better than me, I have accepted that!"

ME (TO LAURA)

I've noticed when most people talk about their spouses or their children, they talk a lot about them being the "best." I may have even done that in this series of essays. If I did, please scold me later. It's most evident when people say, "My wife (or husband) is my *best friend!*" Personally, I have a hard time saying that, not because Laura is not an outstanding friend. She is a fantastic listener, a giving person, and someone that people seek out to spend time with. She is probably the par-excellence of what a friend is like, but I don't categorize her as my best friend for several reasons. First, marriage is different than a friendship—marriage is a lot deeper and carries much more responsibility than a friendship—it is just a different thing altogether. In addition, saying she is my friend would put her in competition with my other friends. I don't want to do that because there is no need or value in that comparison. What she is should be different from friendship instead of subservient to friendship. And last, as good as she is at being a friend, she is much better at being a wife and partner to me. I don't want to give that up so that we can be just "buddies."

Maybe the more appropriate thing to articulate is who is she? She makes my life more interesting and fuller and exciting than it would be without her. My first trip to Taiwan was completely different than the second because she was now with me. This second adventure was truly an adventure and Laura made the trip leading up to and including the Tea Shop more of something I will never forget.

One thing that is evident about Laura is her compassion. I saw it when I had my scooter accident. When I see someone hurting or if I saw them fly over the handlebars of a scooter, I would first think, "Man, that was pretty cool!" Then I would gather my thoughts and think, "Wait, I'm supposed to be compassionate, let me think of something compassionate to say." Laura is different from that. When she saw me flying across greater Taiwan and skid across the pavement, she literally felt with me and automatically let out a gasp of compassion. When we watch football, she can cheer against the other team for only so long until her compassion builds up and she feels sorry for them. We can't watch anything on tv where people get hurt because she seems to feel what they feel.

Laura also follows the rules. When we were on the wrong train headed South, I could see it in her eyes. My son and I were a little excited because we got to ride the more expensive train for a cheaper price. Sometimes pushing the envelope is kind of exciting! There was hardly anyone on the train, at first, and it was exciting waiting for them to eventually "bust" us. However, I could tell that Laura didn't feel the same way. I could see her thinking, "They're going to find out, this is so bad, we're breaking the rules!" People like me need people like Laura that are committed to keeping the rules. It keeps me in check when I'm looking for excitement and sometimes being rebellious. People like Laura bring an order to the world that is necessary for the rest of us. And, personally I think it helps me most because I can be a little selfish. Rules are generally designed to help us be cognizant of other people and how we affect them. Laura knows this instinctually!

Laura doesn't settle for mediocre. What this means is that she doesn't allow herself to accept "this is as good as it's ever going to get." I credit much of our personal growth to her dissatisfaction with the status quo. This has always kept me striving to be better because she raises the bar when I am drifting toward mediocrity instead of striving for the better.

The reason I bring this up is because her voice is the one that I heard that made me sit down and listen to the man with no name. I could hear her encouragement to listen to him, and be present, to take some time and enjoy this moment. I hear her voice when people are being hurtful—I tend to absorb it where she softly encourages me to move on and find some better friends. My children are mostly the people they are because Laura very judiciously taught them not to settle for less than the best!

In the pictures of the Tea Shop adventure from chapter 5, Tanya snapped the picture where we all look delighted with the man with no name. This is slightly misleading; I tend to fade in and out of delight when things impress me or bore me. At the Tea Shop, there was a lot to captivate my attention that night, so I probably did pretty good. But Laura seems to be totally present with people in a way that is mesmerizing. I watch her out of the corner of my eye respond to people and I marvel at the intensity of it. Often, she declines to get together with people, and I think I know the reason why. I think she is so present and empathetic and compassionate toward people that she becomes exhausted when we spend time around others. I love my grandchildren and children and I'm interested in how people work, but Laura genuinely delights in people and engages them! She is the most compassionate, empathic person that I know!

Sometimes men and women tease each other about emotions and we make fun of our emotionalism in whatever ways it's expressed. When I tell people that I am excited, they say, "Really, I can't tell—you have the same expression when you are sad as when you are excited." When Laura is excited or sad or mad or glad or disappointed, you know it! I could make fun of her being Italian and Irish, but it's more of just who she is. If there's anything I naturally delight in without being coached, it is this: I genuinely love that her feelings and emotions are not pushed down into the shadows. When we began to truly experience the Tea Shop, it came out in Laura's expressions, words, and actions. I'm sure the man with no name felt it—Tanya probably felt it – and I drew energy from it. Of course, it's taken me months to draw those feelings out and, being me, of course I have to analyze them and study them. Laura just simply felt them that night and I admire that!

After being a pastor for 20 years, plus being alive for a half century, I have seen a lot of marriages. Some of them I saw just from the storefronts that they displayed to the public and others I have seen from the dirty, neglected storage rooms way deep on the inside. There are no golden, problem-free marriages. Marriages are messy, complicated, mysterious, and frustrating—but marriage is also beautiful. In thirty years, Laura and I have been through many highs and lows. We have grown and slid backward and recommitted and been frustrated. To call our marriage a rollercoaster would be to classify it tamely in some seasons. Here is what it boils down to for me: Laura is not my best friend and I don't want to even start all that "best" language as I mentioned earlier.

Laura is the person that sits across the table from me and considers the next step. The next step is often scary or uncertain or, sometimes, exciting! We both have doubts and sometimes we even doubt each other. Occasionally, we make "pro" and "con" lists and try to properly analyze things before we throw up our hands and say, "I don't know." After we've cried and laughed and prayed and got the best advice we possibly can, Laura looks deep into my eyes, and after the inevitable pause of consideration, she says, "*Okay. Let's...*

"...get married!"

"...have a baby!"

"...go back to college!"

"... go to Taiwan!"

"...go find a teapot!"

"...do this thing together!"

I don't know if either of us is the best at anything, but we've done a lot of stuff together and most of it turned out pretty good. It's been scary and messy and fun and exciting and chocked full of highs and lows but the thing that is *best* about it all is not how well it turned out. The thing that I love most about her is not that she always agrees with me or serves me or even makes me happy, because, let's face it; she often makes me feel angry! What I love most about Laura is that after all the deliberation and consideration and even consternation, eventually we look into each other's eyes and say, "Let's do this!"

真知灼見

Some Deeper Lessons

WHERE IS GOD?

"Here there is no Gentile or Jew, circumcised or uncircumcised barbarian, Scythian, slave or free, but Christ is all, and is in all".

THE APOSTLE PAUL

Occasionally, my dog Winston reminds me of who he is and most of the time that irritates me. Just a few minutes ago, he nudged me when he wanted me to go in a different direction. I yell at him, "One day you are going to knock me down!" He just looks at me. He's a Miniature Australian Shepherd and it's just what they do. His breed likes to make sure they know where everyone in the house is and they are most at peace when the herd is all in one place. When more than three people are over, he is a hot mess—we have to put him in the bedroom because he drives everyone crazy. He also barks when he is outside to let us know that people, he hasn't approved of yet, are coming into our "area." He seems to be saying, "Just thought I'd let you know that they were out there—cause I'm not sure what they are doing in our area, ya know—just thought I'd let you know!" When I yell at him, he just stares at me. It's what he does.

I hate to compare God to my dog, but I would like to think God works in similar ways sometimes. My experience in the Tea Shop raised some very big questions for me. Like Winston, God seemed to be nudging me to change direction or alerting me to something I had never considered. That bothers me a little. I have become more open over the years to other trains of thought, but a part of me still likes being certain about everything and knowing exactly what I believe. I was deeply moved by my experience in the Tea Shop, but I have been contemplating what happened for several months now. Really, it just started with a question. After experiencing this man with no name in the Tea Shop, I began to mull over the question, "Where was God?" Every indicator I have says God was in that guy in the Tea Shop even though he most likely was not a Christian. However, I saw every fruit of the Spirit exhibited in him. How could this be? What was the explanation?

Dr. Paul nudged me this morning when he posed the question in a different way, "Where is God not present?" Imagine me muttering to myself and wandering around my house with *that* question spinning around in my little brain. Is that my dog barking outside again? *I think I'll just go out and join him.*

Where is God not present is a good question—No, that's a great question! (David reflects on this thought in Psalm 139). If God were to choose a place or a person to not inhabit, who or what would that be? In the United States, we often assume that we are exceptional, and that God somehow favors us, especially those that feel they have the "right" beliefs. But even if that were true, wouldn't God be more interested in being with the less favored child than the one that already has it figured out? Wouldn't God be most active in the "shit-hole" places that need His wisdom and compassion? Or does God wait for me to carry Him to those places? Was He only in the Tea Shop because I was there? I don't think so! I got the impression that this man was experiencing something he was familiar with, and I was the one that was blown away.

So, is God in everything? Another friend just suggested that maybe a better question is "Where is love?" Yeah, that's another fantastic question! I'm going to start cussing soon. Oops, I already did! This is really upsetting my apple cart. God is love, so wherever love is would seem to be where God is. There's a lot of references in the Bible to Christ being in us and in all things— it's kind of hard to ignore, but every person from my previous religious life seems to be pretty good at it (Ignoring it, that is!). We seemed to be good at classifying people as "other." Richard Rohr kind of nudged me towards that one. When I recognize something God-like in that person, it gets harder to classify them differently than myself. I saw God "in" him! What I know to be God seemed to be there and in him. Was he just possessed by God for a moment? It didn't appear that he was caught off guard. And what would be the purpose of that anyway? My old tradition would say that I need to convince him, not the other way around.

I understand just a little bit of Celtic Spirituality and often even less about what I hear when I listen to Richard Rohr. The article[1] I read today from Rohr and what I know about Celtic

1 https://cac.org/how-can-everything-be-sacred-2018-01-02/

Spirituality nudges me toward the idea of everything being sacred. When thinkers talk about the true self and that when we get beyond the container (or wineskin) of our false self, they describe what is called the *true* self and generally they see God there! When people talk about consciousness, are they really talking about knowledge of God or just characteristics of God? Does it even matter? Can you separate God from His nature? Are we closer in our beliefs than we are apart? And, if God is in creation, is there a part of it that He is not in?

I don't think the guy in the Tea Shop was God, but I think God was in him! To be honest, that creates more questions than answers. But somehow, it seems to be nudging me closer to the truth. Winston never tackles me or tugs on my clothes like the guard dogs in the movies. I appreciate that about him, although I still must admit that like the nudges from others, it still ticks me off. My false self seems to resist the necessary growth that must happen for me to learn what is true. I don't want questions, I want answers, but I must admit that I have drifted off course or maybe I didn't ever know where I was going in the first place. What I do love is that these nudges and questions seem to be leading me to something more beautiful even if everything in me wants to resist.

So, now just picture me wandering off into the recesses of my house, cursing under my breath but occasionally stopping to look up and exclaim, "ohhh, hmmm!" I want to blame it on Winston again, but he's already drifted off to sleep on the floor. Maybe I can teach him to talk... nah, that would probably just tick me off even more. I'd probably see God in him. I think I need to go lay down.

THE PRACTICE

"..as was His custom.."

LUKE 4:16

The events in the Tea Shop are hard to put into chronological order. I can't recall the exact time when the owner of the Tea Shop stood up and demonstrated what Tanya described as his "practice." I think it was just after we began to share tea and before his wife brought out the already described delicious food. To be clear, the nameless man was not describing his beliefs—he was sharing with us his *practice*. In one of the pictures, Tanya captured him holding his hands in a certain way. Shortly after this, he interlocked his fingers and then twisted them in the most interesting way. If you ever attended Sunday School as a kid then you may remember doing something similar with your hands where you twisted them around while you rhymed, "Here's the church, here's the steeple...", it was kind of like that but much more complex. He went on to do a sort of prayer pose, but his hands were behind his shoulders instead of in front—I think I pulled a muscle just thinking about it.

Later, he also demonstrated balance by standing on one leg on a stool and doing something similar to what Ralph Macchio did in the movie, *Karate Kid*. It was impressive to see a sixty-year-old balancing like that. I was impressed and was more than ready for him to offer to sell me a book or DVD on his *practice*. I would actually have paid top dollar for it—here was living proof that it worked. His practice was effective, and I wanted some of that in my life. However, the DVD offer didn't come, he just returned to making tea for us. This was his personal practice, influenced by his teacher, probably a long time ago. He was excited about it, but it was personal and not something that could be learned from a DVD or book.

The first thing that I noticed from my friend in the Tea Shop is that practices are both prescriptive and personal. There was an element of the practice that had been "passed down" to him but also there was an ownership of the practice as his own personal journey. Tanya told us his mentor taught him this practice, but she described it as "*His*" practice, personal and intimate to him and no one else. The New Testament uses a Greek word, *ethos*, to describe the practices of Jesus, Paul, and the people of that time.[2] *Ethos* is a word describing character—the beliefs and ideals of a people group. I think there is always the element of what we inherit (what's been passed down or taught to us) in our *practice* and what we make personal in our *practice* (how we work that out day to day). Jesus went up to the temple, but also went out in solitude to pray. His "Spirit and Truth"[3] admonition

---

2 Luke 4:16, Acts 17:2, 1 Corinthians 15:33, Hebrews 10:25
3 John 4:24

to the woman with questions seemed to indicate that although practices are passed down to us, they can also change over time.

My personal practice has evolved somewhat because of the nameless man. I was raised with very little structure—no liturgy or practice really except that we were told to read the Bible. I was also taught to go to church and to pray. I have found some value in things like "well-crafted prayers"[4] and liturgies that follow the church calendar. I have incorporated the ancient practice of centering prayer, along with yoga and meditation. The writing that I do is a part of my practice. It helps me understand what I think, clarifies my thoughts, and helps me crystallize my intentions. Some people do this in a journal.

I remember he was excited about his practice. His face lit up like a schoolboy during show-and-tell as he spoke and demonstrated how effective his practice was in his life. There was no doubt he believed in his practice, I believe he was committed to it and would most likely share it with anyone. People often get a little irritated because I want to talk to them about how I am a vegan. Just like this man's practice, being vegan has done so much for me that I often fight the urge to talk about it. I get excited to share about it with others. Veganism has reversed many of my health issues. I feel better and I believe in it! Speaking of beliefs, the man with no name didn't talk about his core beliefs at all. He didn't try to "evangelize" us or share his gospel with us—he shared his practice with us. That meant so much more to

---

4   This is a term I learned from Brian Zahnd to describe using prayer books and ancient prayers.

me than a set of principles or beliefs I had to subscribe to. I was curious about his beliefs because he shared his practice with us.

I am sure his practice had some spiritual elements to it as it is very hard to separate the spiritual and the physical. I understand them to be intricately connected, but he focused on sharing with us the physical dimensions of his practice. I have seen people in religious circles who have made fun of anything related to physical practice. In Christian circles, it is confusing how the body is labeled as a temple, but we also see it as something dirty or defiled. We call it a temple but then we don't treat it with respect. This man was approximately 60 years old, yet he moved like a teenager. I didn't get the impression that he worshipped his body like a bodybuilder might, but most of his practice was centered around caring for his temple. I don't know if that's what he called it, but he certainly treated it that way.

This care for his body even included his diet. It is evident in Asian countries that there is a lot less obesity and disease. However, this is changing in countries like China where they have heavily imported American food and made other socioeconomic changes.[5] Before I delve off into a rant about the benefits of a plant-based diet, suffice it to say that part of our practice should be the care and nurture of our "temple" as it serves as a vehicle to transport and interact with the more spiritual parts of us. I have seen too many people claiming to be spiritual who laugh at people that care to have a practice of fostering good health. Laura and I have experienced behavior bordering on abuse in church basements because we changed the way we ate

5 https://www.ncbi.nlm.nih.gov/pmc/articles/PMC2939400/

to improve our health. My friend in the Tea Shop found that he could do both—he was able to tend to his body and his soul through effective *practice*.

Since he didn't have a DVD, I probably won't adopt his practice. If we lived close together, maybe I could learn more from him and that might be something I could incorporate into my practice. But, for now, it's enough to observe and implement the things that I have inherited from my faith. Then, as I come to understand God and myself better, I can implement the practices that foster a body and soul that is healthy and vibrant and connected. I still read the Scriptures, but I am learning to see it in a different light. It's not something I do or check off the list like a prescription handed out at a conference or a counseling session. I still pray but in a deeper, fuller way. My new practices don't replace my old practices, they have enhanced them.

I would love to give you a prescribed list of practices that would spur you on to success. But all I can do is be an example, like the guy in the Tea Shop, and hope that you will discover what works best for you. If I ever do discover something I can put on YouTube, I definitely will. I suspect we will just have to journey together and discover more as we go further. Practice, practice, practice until we find peace and awareness within.

EVANGELISM

"Take nothing with you..."

JESUS

The most memorable spiritual night of my life happened when absolutely no beliefs were discussed, no faith was shared, no prayers were offered, and no debates were had. I believe everyone is driven by belief and we want everyone else to believe in it too (a Christian word called "evangelism"). I imagine part of the reason we want to share our beliefs with others is because whatever we have believed in has *saved* us in some way. I know this because I feel that way about my plant-based lifestyle. I feel a vegan lifestyle has saved my life and restored my health—this was good news for me. Naturally, I want to share that story with others. I admit that early on I was too zealous, and I made some people mad because my arguments tended to be aggressive. I was a little too strong about sharing my good news. I was the same way about the good news of my faith (better known in Christian circles as "the gospel"). I admit that early in my faith I felt like I had to convince people of my beliefs. Later, I was taught that it was my duty and responsibility to convince people and behold, an evangelist was born!

Religious beliefs did not surface in the Tea Shop. Normally, I would have thought about how to *convert* this person, but that night I didn't give it a second thought. In retrospect, I believe we did more to share our separate faith with each other by not thinking about it than if we would have been very direct and tried to convince each other who was right and wrong. What I am discovering is that evangelism is more about being what you believe than explaining what you believe. As I mentioned before, because we were in his home territory, the man with no name was able to share his practice with me (and that blessed me), but our beliefs were never mentioned. It is profound to me that one of the most memorable spiritual nights of my life happened with absolutely no discussion of our beliefs. We simply were what we believed we should be and that was enough!

Recently my friend, Keith Giles, shared with me research concerning Millennials from Barna Research.[6] The research showed that millennials are confident about sharing their faith, but believe less in evangelism. What was most interesting about this research is that Millennials have 3-4 times more non-Christians friends than any other generation group previously. This proves that they're more willing to love people outside their faith circle. In my previous book and in recent blog posts, I have expressed how the younger generation (especially my children's generation) is influencing my beliefs. Millennials seem to know

---

6 https://www.patheos.com/blogs/keithgiles/2019/02/barna-poll-millennial-christians-have-more-non-christian-friends/

instinctively what I discovered in the Tea Shop - sharing my faith is about sharing my life. Drawing from the Barna Research-to share my life with others, I have to spend time with more friends who think differently than I do. It seems almost counter-intuitive, but we are able to influence *more* people simply by living and sharing our lives with them instead of trying to *save* them.

Let's come full circle here; the evangelical ideals originated from the Greek word *evangelio* which is usually translated *gospel* and means *good news*. Originally, this was the announcement that Jesus is Lord and not Caesar. However, over time it became a sales pitch to get people into our individual belief system. I think many Evangelicals today are still in love with Caesar and the old empire, especially those Evangelicals that have grown up in the United States. The good news was not ever meant to be, "my religion is better than your religion." Jesus came to inaugurate a new Kingdom of peace and mercy and love and that's good news!

Jesus said, "Take nothing with you," and I think he was trying to tell us to go live our lives in a way that impacts people. Love God and love one another. Stop being violent and depending on violence to bring peace. Let the peace of God dwell in your hearts and let them see your good works. You can't change the world by huddling together and then occasionally marching out to try to convince people. That is not what makes disciples. Be what you believe and argue less, love your neighbor, bless those who persecute you, be at peace with all people—that is what saves the world!

My old tradition hinted at these ideas but couldn't quite commit to doing life together. It didn't quite work on the church planter's progress report to report that we broke bread together with "non-believers" and that was the main activity we did this month. I felt that we were always searching for a more impressive strategy and a new approach. In the end, we just seemed to always be recruiting new people for churches that were slowly emptying out. It was more like a multi-level marketing scheme than what Jesus seemed to be talking about.

I am committed to doing exactly what I experienced in the Tea Shop. I want to be present with people every day. I want to spend time with people, I want to hear their struggles, I want to share their joys, and I want them to tell me about their practices. When I visit someone, instead of sharing my beliefs with them I want to share my practices. My beliefs will ultimately be demonstrated in the way I live. The most important beliefs, like love God and love my neighbor, can only be demonstrated in love - they cannot be explained without application. In reality, the only effective evangelism technique is to love my neighbor as myself. That pretty much solves every problem in the world and says everything we need to say about what we believe.

BYPASSING

"What you resist, persists." [7]

C. G. JUNG

I started eating a vegan diet three years ago. The reasons weren't entirely ethical: at age 50, I was beginning to have some worrisome health issues just like my father and grandfather. To make it even more relevant, my brother-in-law dropped dead of a heart condition while at the gym working out at age 48. Both my father and grandfather had heart episodes and later had bypass surgery. Bypass surgery is where a surgeon cuts open your chest, spreads the ribs and uses a vein from the leg to *bypass the* blocked artery or arteries in the heart. Read that again. This very expensive surgery does nothing to solve the issue other than subvert or bypass it for a short time. My father and grandfather are witness to that since they died shortly after. Bypassing the issue does not solve the root causes of that issue, it just makes a person feel better until the issue reappears in different ways or in

---

7 https://clarity.zone/what-you-resist-persists-but-what-did-jung-really-mean-by-this/

different parts of the body. I think a lot of us do this spiritually where we *bypass* the real problem when indicators present issues in our life.

Robert Augustus Masters talks about this in his book, *Spiritual Bypassing,* "[Spiritual Bypassing is] the use of spiritual beliefs to avoid dealing with painful feelings, unresolved wounds and developmental needs." A *spiritual bypass* or *spiritual bypassing* then is a "tendency to use spiritual ideas and practices to sidestep or avoid facing unresolved emotional issues, psychological wounds, and unfinished developmental tasks"[8] As a pastor, and as a participant in many churches, I have seen this consistently and in churches of all shapes and sizes. Just like we have an epidemic of heart disease that we are treating with surgical bypass, so too we have an epidemic of internal and unresolved emotional wounds that we are spiritually avoiding with our ideas and practices. When we get stressed, we default to spiritual languages and practices to avoid dealing with the real issue. Often, I would resort to my spiritual language and practice to deflect dealing with the issues I really needed to. It's kind of like a suit of armor meant to deflect any real examination.

Being in the Tea Shop brought down these guards. Some of my close friends at Heart Connexion Ministries like to emphasize we need to have experiences that get us past the watchful dragons in our lives that keep us from growing. Spiritual bypassing is a defense that we have to subvert to get to the root of our issues. The language barrier of the Tea Shop distracted me long enough to experience some real intimacy and get past my

---

8   https://en.wikipedia.org/wiki/Spiritual_bypass

fears of communing with someone different than me. It would have been easy to spiritualize the experience and avoid the intimate contact with the man with no name by saying spiritual things like, *"It felt kind of dark in there..."* or *"I had a check in my spirit..."* So often I'm guilty of telling people, *"I will pray for you."*, instead of truly listening or sitting with them. I used to feel all "spiritual" even though I avoided the very experience that might have brought healing. I suppose many of us have defense mechanisms like this and label them as spiritual. What usually is true about those types of situations is that I am simply afraid or unsure of myself—it's not really a spiritual problem at all but I make it out to be one so I don't have to deal with my own insecurities and issues.

Later, the man with no name asked what year we were born. We discovered Laura and I were both born in the year of the dragon. It didn't take much to convince us to buy some beautiful little dragon statues. They were painted gold and were exquisitely handcrafted. Now that the statues are in my house, they serve a couple of purposes for me. First, they help me remember the Tea Shop experience and the people we interacted with that night. Second, the dragons remind me of my proclivity to bypass real intimacy and true healing when I allow my *watchful dragons* to deflect what should occur.

Genuine community, even if it is halfway around the world, is where I find healing. I have learned that I am often wounded in community. When hearts connect and experience each other with an attitude of grace and acceptance, I find healing. As long as I avoid the urge to bypass, I can do the deep work that only comes in community with others. A man with no name from the other side of the world that spoke a different language and practiced another religion brought healing to my soul and life to my practices because the situation dictated that we didn't have time to bypass the necessary.

Physically, I am much better now thanks to my whole-food plant-based diet and moderate exercise. I recently had a stress test and performed admirably. I am slowly reversing my heart disease. I have no guarantees that I will be without complications, but the outlook is a lot better now.

Spiritually speaking, I am healthier.

I have worked very hard not to bypass the spiritual and emotional issues in my life with spiritual language that doesn't really solve the problem. I am learning to "sit" with problems and own them instead of trying to bypass them. I am learning to empathize with people instead of trying to find a quick solution to their issues. Sometimes life just "sucks" and we need to admit that and face it. I am learning to truly listen to the hearts of those that cross my path instead of fixing them or promising them what is not true. Even when I sound spiritual, I stop and ask whether I am bypassing the hard work that really needs to take place.

Eating better, exercising, and implementing better practices in my life has taken hard work. I have had to be disciplined and change my diet, but It would be harder to have open heart surgery. Similarly, it is hard to work through my heart issues in community, but it is much harder when those same wounds fester and become more established in my soul. I am happy that

I am finding communities that help promote genuine focus on my *heart* issues instead of communities that bypass and avoid root causes. I am finding the courage to step into situations like the Tea Shop and get past my watchful dragons.

UNKNOWING

"Paradoxically, the challenges of our day-to-day exis-
tence are substantial reminders that our life of faith
simply must have its center somewhere other than in
our ability to hold it together in our minds." [9]

PETER ENNS

Currently, I am transitioning between jobs. This is the first time in 25 years that I have been without regular employment. I have three options in front of me that are totally different from any profession that I've done before. For whatever reason, I feel confident moving forward and stepping into the unknown. All of the options have about the same level of uncertainty—all of them have pros and cons. There doesn't seem to be a logical path. The choice that seemed the most logical just got a little more complicated. This entire journey to set myself on a new path has challenged my faith—faith in myself, faith in God, and faith in other people.

---

9 Peter Enns, *The Sin of Certainty*, Kindle Version, p. 118

When I walked into the Tea Shop, I didn't have time to be logical. The whole experience happened so quickly that my normal defenses didn't kick in fast enough. I often feel paralyzed by analysis but that wasn't available to me as a trusted resource in the Tea Shop. I had no frame of reference to make an analysis. The Tea Shop served as a metaphor for me in stepping into the unknown. Almost everything about this experience (except the tofu and the sunflower seeds) was something that I had never experienced. Even then, the tofu was not my *brand* of tofu and was varied and unique. My mind didn't have time to regulate my actions to what was safe or what was "normal." Adventures are like that sometimes. Merriam-Webster defines an adventure as "an undertaking usually involving danger and unknown risks."[10] So, by definition, adventures can't be totally calculated or known in advance. Adventures most certainly are not safe.

I am coming to understand that this stepping into the unknown is not only valuable, but necessary. Most of the time I travel down well-worn paths of familiarity. I want safe adventures, but *safe adventures* are a contradiction in terms.

I have always loved my analytical, pragmatic certainty. I liked knowing what I know and being sure about it. I am learning, in matters of journey and adventure and belief, that it is just as important to forget what you know as it is to know what you know. For example, it is probable that our view of God is flawed. There are hundreds, if not thousands, of Christians groups that all believe they are right about God. And guess what? It is likely

---

10 https://www.merriam-webster.com/dictionary/adventure

that all of us are wrong. It is only when we "unknow" that our minds open to learn something new.

In the past, I would have approached the Tea Shop with a certainty that I knew what I needed to do. Even though I am a little shy because I knew what I knew and was certain about it, my ego would carry me through trying to sell them on whatever my latest belief was. It's a common malady that affects us all— We love to be certain.

So far, I have recalled approximately 13 lessons that I learned from the Tea Shop that I believe will change my life in one way or another. Even the best seminars usually only have one or two *takeaways* or *nuggets* that I could use to improve my journey. It has been nine months and I am still unpacking the beneficial lessons from the man with no name. Actually, I finally discovered that his name is known, but it's a little difficult to write in English and it doesn't really matter at this point anyways… and I think we all like a little mystery and intrigue so I'll leave it for now. Could it be true that knowing always requires some level of unknowing? When we give up our death grip on certainty, we open the door expanding our understanding and deepening our consciousness. I know it is scary, but good adventures tend to be like that.

TIME

"I used to be afraid of failing at something that really mattered to me, but now I'm more afraid of succeeding at things that don't matter." [11]

BOB GOFF

I am good at estimating how long it will take to do something, and, with a little planning, I can get a lot of things done in the time span of a day. I try not to feel like I'm *running late* or *wasting time* because one of my chief aims in life is to make the most of every day. When I see time as a river, where I don't ever get the time back, I assume I should make every moment count and accomplish as much as I can every day. This has been my philosophy since...well little Karl (also known as Joey) was learning to walk. Most people would see me as a good manager of time. For most of my life that has been one of my highest aspirations.

Recently, I was introduced online to a pastor starting a new church. Someone thought we might have some things in common. He and his wife were about to have their first church service

---

11 Bob Goff, *Love Does: Discover a Secretly Incredible Life in an Ordinary World*

and he was busy with the preparations. I couldn't go to the first service, so I reached out to him about a week later. Already, after just a week of operation, this young pastor was so busy that he didn't seem to have the time to see me. Years ago, I would have been hurt, but I think I understand now. The problem, as I see it, is that he has either packed his schedule full of *good* things to do so that he feels useful and necessary and productive or he is a poor time manager and situations and struggles are controlling him. It's the tyranny of the urgent and balance of our ego that flings us into these epic battles.

The first half of my life was dominated by my ego, which is not necessarily a bad thing. I had a certain amount of need to establish my career and identity and I longed to provide for my family. Sounds pretty good, right? During this part of my life, I tried to *invest* time in value-added activities. Just like I sought to invest my money into companies that pay dividends, I tried to invest my time in the most productive activities that would form the *container* of my life as described by Richard Rohr.

> "Thus, the first part of the spiritual journey is about externals, formulas, superficial emotions, flags and badges, correct rituals, Bible quotes, and special clothing, all of which largely substitute for an actual spiritual journey (see Matthew 23:13-32). Yet they are all used and needed to create the container."[12]

In his book, *Falling Upward*, Rohr talks about a second half of life where it is possible to live different and pursue different goals. I feel like I began my second half of life after my deconstruction a few years ago. Since that time, situations like the Tea

12   https://cac.org/the-container-and-the-contents-2016-06-19/

Shop have taught me to think differently about a number of things, including how I think about time. Is time really a river that is flowing by where I have to spend the moments as quickly and efficiently as possible? Or is time like a wallet of minutes and hours that I must spend each day—an investment portfolio that I shuffle each day, hoping for the greatest return? Quite possibly is it something I should think less logically about and just let it pass through my hands as I enjoy the journey. Those are just some of the questions and assumptions that philosophers and poets and prophets have wrestled with throughout time.

The writer of Proverbs in the Bible gave several ideas about time that somewhat relate to this point and, believe it or not, appear to contradict each other.[13] This is not a new struggle. As I grow old, and hopefully mature, I am starting to discover something better than time management. I am learning that there are segments of time which do more for me than just help me make more money or improve my reputation or whatever metric makes the most sense to me today. I would call these life-changing moments. For example, the birth of a child. My wife was in labor for 14 hours with our first child—not very efficient—but, this was a life-altering moment. The Tea Shop turned out to be one of those moments for me as well.

I will admit that because of my influence, the first part of the trip to Taiwan was well organized and intended to efficiently guide us to fun and relaxation at a reasonable price. However, almost every aspect of the first part of the trip that I time-managed *blew up* in one way or another. We had to walk from the

13 Proverbs 16:9, Proverbs 21:5, Proverbs 27:1

airport to the first hotel, which wasn't reserved properly so we had to walk to another hotel. Up until the time when we finally went hiking, something we didn't plan, the trip was really a series of planned disasters. And, if I was honest, from a time-management standpoint, it was a failure. But, looking back, I remember all the things I didn't plan like our cab ride to the hotel and the daily trips to the vegetable stand and, finally, the 4-hour hike at the gorge.

Eventually, this series of unfortunate events led us to the Tea Shop which was probably the biggest lesson and blessing of all for that trip. Up to that point in time, I never spent more than 10 minutes buying anything except a car and a house in my entire life. The two hours we would invest in the people we met in the Tea Shop (and we will probably never meet again) changed my life. But what was fundamentally important about this time?

When Jesus said, "Love your neighbor as yourself,"[14] I think he was encouraging us to spend our time making people feel valued, accepted, and appreciated. That is exactly what the people in the Tea Shop did for me. They took a segment of their day, devoted it to me, and caused my life to change dramatically. Recently, I thought about how many tasks they could have gotten done in that span of time. For starters, they could have cleaned the shop up and organized the shelves. That's time-management 101, right? They could have spent time organizing their inventory, sweeping the floor a bit, getting new marketing in place, getting supper ready, etc. What I am discovering though is that not all *timewasters* are actually a waste of time. Maybe

---

14 Mark 12:31

people that are so efficient are really just feeding their immature egos and not really doing the things that matter most.

I'm sure that we will always have things that we have to do. Eating, sleeping, and taking care of the essentials are probably things we shouldn't avoid. However, I think we can keep those things in perspective and give some priority to the non-tangibles that promote the greatest commandments (love God, love others). I hope that I am learning the value of finding things that matter more than efficiency. Everyone has had the experience of doing something and saying, "I'll never get that time back." But, if I'm honest, I realize that most of those events were when people were using me for their own gain, and I wonder how often I have done the same to others.

I just had another experience this past weekend with my Heart Connexion Community. I got to be a training assistant during the Breakthrough seminar. Altogether, I probably spent 40+ hours over the long weekend (not to mention the added hours driving just to get there). I took time away from my family and we even had to put the dog in a kennel because Laura was participating in part of the weekend as well. We were able to show love to the participants and I received blessings on many levels. It didn't help my career or my reputation and fiscally it was costly for me, but it will be a time I will never forget, and I will look back on it with only good memories.

My new goal in life is not to manage my time. What I am searching for now is not a good career move or wealth builder or crowd-pleasing management of events. What I am now striving for is to stumble into as many life-changing experiences as I can.

I guess that's why we call it a *journey* and I'm sure that is why it's known as an *adventure*. My eyes are wide-open, but my heart is also searching for opportunities to see the Tea Shop experiences when they present themselves and not sacrifice them on the altar of time management and efficiency.

INVINCIBLE PRECIOUSNESS

When I go walking, occasionally I will see something that catches my attention. These are not any particular things that I look for, rather they're something out of the ordinary that causes me to want to investigate further. If I am walking, I make a mental note of it and circle back to it later to discover exactly what it is. I really don't have favorite things to look for, I'm just curious about everything. Unfortunately, sometimes it happens while I'm listening to a speech or reading a book and I must refocus myself. That is sort of what happened when I was listening to a lecture by my friend, Dr. Paul Fitzgerald.

He just kind of snuck it into the conversation. I may have heard him say it before, and it sounded sort of familiar, but I had to circle back to learn more about this interesting term. The wording felt good, it sounded like something I wanted; but unfortunately, I forgot about it as soon as my mind chased some other butterfly. Yesterday, I thought about the phrase again, so I asked a couple of my friends and Dr. Paul if they could explain it to me. I talked with my Spiritual Director about it and she seemed like she was familiar with it and helped me unpack it

further—she's good like that. This is what I have come to understand about *invincible preciousness*.

My friend Peggy was the first to speak up. She's like that and
I love that she is honest and transparent about what is on her
mind. She explained, "I understand invincible preciousness to
be that deep place in us that cannot be sullied by our sin, bro-
kenness, and wounding. We are never at risk of losing our preciousness before God."

Oh man, isn't that beautiful? Another friend, Rachel,
described invincible preciousness as "coming to terms with
God's constant, loving gaze on me (or in me)." She admits that
this initially made her anxious and vulnerable, but now feels
warm and loved by the thought of it. Dr. Paul explained that
although we may wander from the love of God, the image and
likeness of God in us "is never marred by anything that happens
to us... and, we carry a felt sense of the Christ that is in us."

Richard Rohr tells a story of his colleague, James Finley, who
realized these things while dealing with suffering.[15] He states, "It
is in the midst of this turning that we discover the qualitatively
richer, more vulnerable place is actually the abyss-like, loving
presence of God, welling up and giving itself in and as the intimate interiority of our healing journey. When we risk sharing
what hurts the most in the presence of someone who will not
invade us or abandon us, we unexpectedly come upon within
ourselves what Jesus called the pearl of great price: the invincible
preciousness of ourselves in our fragility." Wow, to me, that is
significant!

---

15 https://cac.org/invincible-preciousness-2018-10-24/

Rohr stresses that when we are vulnerable and share what we think will kill us in one way or another, "…we unexpectedly come upon within ourselves this invincible love that sustains us unexplainably in the midst of the painful situation we are in." In other words, we feel our invincible preciousness. As we learn to trust the gaze of God, it touches the hurting places and begins to dissolve the hurt until all that is left is love.

Of all places, I found this invincible preciousness in the Tea Shop, even though the people there could not have articulated it any better than I could. It wasn't necessary for them to understand it to get it! In a gradual way, when I am able to accept love and kindness and respect from others, I am able to recognize what I carry in my body—this felt sense of Christ and our invincible preciousness before God. Dr. Paul also encouraged me to investigate what might be blocking my awareness of this preciousness and give up control so that I might learn to live in the beauty of this truth.

I know what you're thinking—It's such a deep thought! But this is one of those things that is worth pursuing. I think the people in the Tea Shop thought it was, they seemed like they had a sense of this preciousness. In this way, I hope I can be more like them—I hope one day I can understand very deeply, like my friends, this invincible preciousness. I did not give much advice in this book, because this was my journey. But, I encourage you to explore this idea of invincible preciousness. Even if you just explore it in solitude, you will be happy you did!

THE LITTLE THINGS

I just got in from taking the dog out. I try to do my fair share with the little things around the house. Laura always comes out to be the champ in that area. It seems that I play a lot of games with *the little things*. Over time, little things just do not seem to be that important to me. I know they are necessary, but they just never feel urgent or compelling.

I think the problem is that I love to think about things I haven't done yet. I don't just dream about writing a new blog, I think about writing a best-seller. Instead of looking forward to greeting my wife at the door, I dream about grand vacations and adventures that I'll take her on. Instead of mowing the lawn, I dream about major additions to the house that I don't have the money for. It's almost cliche' to say, "focus on the little things Karl." Even when I want to focus on the little things, I worry that I won't be doing the right things. How will all the pieces fit together? How will it turn out? Is it worth it?

I can't promise to answer any of those questions. But I can tell you from experience worry and concern about big things often keeps me from the little things that get me to that destination. Look at it this way, doing something is getting me closer to something and further away from where I am. Joseph Campbell said, "If you can see your path laid out in front of you step by step, you know it's not your path." Some of us just need to take the next step, own it, and keep looking for clues along the way.

It goes without saying that the guy in the Tea Shop was doing the little things. Without needing to, he braided a little rope on each of the teapots that kept the lid from getting misplaced. It was a little thing, but it was one of the things in the chain of events that led to my conclusions that this was a life-changing event. The fact that I got up this morning and wrote (rewrote) this chapter, is another small thing that may or may not be important, but it felt like a good thing that I could do... so I did it!

May I offer these suggestions?

1. **Do one thing that you already know to do.**
   What is the last thing that you knew you should do and didn't? I think we all get caught up in the details or the 5-year plan or the strategic objectives but don't take a step because the details paralyze us if we think about them all at once. Or we take a step toward it and realize there is a possibility of rejection or it reminds us of a past failure. The idea of failing forward doesn't get enough press. It is almost a requirement that we fail if we are going to succeed. We will never fail by standing still, but we also will never succeed. We don't need to know all the answers, we just need to take a step.

2. Do one thing that scares you.

In the past, I liked to refer to the quote, "Better to remain silent and thought a fool than to speak up and remove all doubt." For years, this kept me comfortable in my cocoon of shyness, at least I didn't look stupid. It wasn't until I started leaning into the discomfort that I realized everything I dreamed about was on the other side of my fear. For some of us it might be confronting a person at work. For others, it might be speaking up when we'd rather be silent. Fear is natural, it sometimes protects us, but we cannot afford to get stranded there in that space. Daily, if not hourly, we should be stepping into our vulnerability and doing something that scares us.

3. Do one thing that brings you joy.

It seems that I often schedule myself so rigorously that I forget to have a little fun. Someone asked me once, "How do you celebrate?" and I told them, "I don't even think I know how!" I dream about vacations or getaways where I will finally be free to relax, but, contrary to the pictures posted on Facebook, many of my retreats are over scheduled and wrought with the same challenges of my daily life—I forget to do the simple things that bring me joy! Only I know what those things are—only I can break the habit of being an adult—only I can allow joy into my routine!

I think it's universal—We all know this, we just forget. When I was a child, I didn't overthink things, I just did what was next in front of me. Now that my prefrontal cortex is all developed and I'm all sophisticated, I forget that little things make a big difference. It's like I feel like I am running out of time and I need to make some big scores, but I forget I can really only do little things—I can't really leap tall buildings in a single bound. But I can climb the first set of stairs leading to the top. There is no instant success. There is no shortcut to the top. There are only little actions and simple thoughts that accumulate into things that are better!

結語

Epilogue

EXPLORING

Several chapters are closing in my life right now. My first book has already been published. For me, writing is a good outlet—it helps me determine what I think and believe. It is refreshing and opening for me to write, but there is also the necessary editing, arranging, and reviewing that is simply hard work. Then, there is the inevitable waiting for each stage of the process—I really struggle with waiting. I have enjoyed my extended transition from one career to another. I had a lot of time to ponder lessons from the Tea Shop and I did a lot of focusing alone to determine what matters most. I am ready to leave the old patterns behind. It is with a twinge of sadness that I leave these things behind, but I also look forward in anticipation.

When I see the final product of my earlier book, I almost look forward to the hard work of refining this one as well. I am looking forward to putting my hands to work at my new career. I am learning that I want to be closer to people, so I expect that this career change will have known and unknown challenges, but it will also give me the chance to grow, develop, and delight in the process. There are several unknowns ahead, who knows what's around the next corner. I may have less time for extracurricular activities and some things may have to change. What I am discovering about myself though, is that I like the journey, the chance to explore.

I like exploring new places. The chance to discover something new or something interesting keeps me moving forward through things that might normally scare me a little. I love to meet new people and see their unique perspective on life because it often teaches me how to navigate the path that I am on. I love studying people and trying to figure out what makes them do what they do. I'm trying to pay attention to the advice of others and "just let it come to me", and just be okay with that.

Rest assured; the next chapter of my life will be an adventure. Some of those adventures I can take from the comfort of my easy chair (Netflix made that easy for everyone), but I think the adventures ahead will necessitate movement and action. I like the idea of contemplation and action and of finding a balance between those two things.

My prayer is that the lessons of the Tea Shop will go with me on this next journey. I pray that my actions and attitude will change to be more like Christ and more like the guy with no name. I am so thankful for those that have journeyed with me. In many ways, they are guides and fellow companions. The journey wouldn't have been the same without them. But I also look forward to the new travelers I will find down the road. I know that they only add to the diversity and excitement of the journey and I can't wait to meet them!

Exploring for me must involve some mystery, a little bit of risk, and a fair amount of companionship. I feel like I'm opening a door into a new dimension. Here's to the next half of my life. Here's to adventure. Here's to exploring what I haven't yet experienced.

Here's to life!

For more information about Karl Forehand

or to contact him for speaking engagements,

please visit *www.desert-sanctuary.com*

Many voices. One message.

Quoir is a boutique publisher
with a singular message: *Christ is all.*
Venture beyond your boundaries to discover Christ
in ways you never thought possible.

For more information, please visit
www.quoir.com